BEYOND THE LODGE
OF THE SUN

BEYOND THE LODGE OF THE SUN

INNER MYSTERIES OF THE
NATIVE AMERICAN WAY

CHOKECHERRY GALL EAGLE

First published by Element Books Ltd 1997
© Vega 2002
Text © Chokecherry Gall Eagle 1997

ISBN 1-84333-631-6

A catalogue record for this book is available
from the British Library

Published in 2002 by
Vega
64 Brewery Road
London, N7 9NT

A member of **Chrysalis** Books plc

Visit our website at www.chrysalisbooks.co.uk

Printed in Wales
by CPD

CONTENTS

ACKNOWLEDGEMENTS 7
DEDICATION 9
INTRODUCTION 13

ONE
SACRED, NOT SECRET...21

TWO
TO GENERATE LIGHT...41

THREE
TWO ROADS, ONE TRUTH...67

FOUR
THE FOUR DIRECTIONS...87

FIVE
HERE AND NOW...109

SIX
USING POWER...121

SEVEN
STONE IS PERCEPTION...151

EIGHT
MEDICINES AND RITUAL...171

NINE
HEALING...191

TEN
WHOLENESS AND ONE-NESS...215

ELEVEN
THE GRAND UNDERSTANDING...231

TWELVE
JESUS AND NATIVE WAYS...249

EPILOGUE 267

ACKNOWLEDGEMENTS

I thank my parents, Elizabeth and Alexander, who let me go my own way, though they did not understand.

I recall and thank my brother, John Alexander, for showing me true courage in the face of death, and life. Rest peacefully, dear brother.

I thank my friends, especially Brian and Myrna, who tried to comfort me through the long, cold years. Their attempts at least gave me hope for warmth if I survived!

I thank my enemies, and laugh; you have only made me stronger.

DEDICATION

This book is dedicated to our grandchildren.

Survival is more than just staying alive. Walk in dignity and Spirit, so that when the fading sun sets for the last time upon your life as a mortal human being, your heart will sing your victories into the ethereal wind, and your soul will know that your struggles have been worthwhile after all.

Mitakuye Oyasin,
all my relatives,
my circle includes all of creation.
Mitakuye Oyasin,
we are all one,
we are also the Great Spirit,
we are the Star Peoples.

INTRODUCTION

I was taught the old ways, yet I was not raised on a reservation. My family lived as much as possible in the dominant western society. Since my earliest memory, I recalled buffalo hunts, and living in a tipi on the central plains at the turn of the 1800s.

When I received my first bow and arrows, I taught my older brother the old childhood games. We would shoot six arrows right up into the air. Then we would stand looking fearlessly into each other's eyes as the razor sharp arrows thudded into the ground all around us.

When I was eleven, I had my visionary experience. From a clear blue sky, a lone thundercloud came racing out of the west. It stopped above me, rumbling. I heard a voice say that I would be taught, but first I would have a dream.

It is from the dream that we derive awareness of our latent spiritual abilities, and any work we might do as part of our learning path.

At the time of my twelfth birthday, I grew seriously ill with double pneumonia. I recall the chills and fever, and then being hospitalized. While in the hospital, I passed in and out of awareness. Lying in bed, I suddenly became very aware and lucid. It seemed that whatever was happening in my body was of little importance. I could sense and feel the world beyond the walls of the room, and I thought I must be dying as my awareness seemed to go further and further beyond those walls.

I found myself standing atop a high mountain, fully aware. I knew that there I was fourteen years old. I looked out cross the land and sky, and absorbed the peacefulness. When I became aware again of my immediate surroundings, I knew that I was now sixteen years old. There was someone standing next to me. I was told many things, including the knowledge of how to go beyond the top of the mountain.

My dream continued, taking me through various ages. Throughout this whole experience, I also knew that I was a twelve-year-old boy lying in a hospital bed.

I saw various people from some distance away. Later in life, I would recognize them as good or bad people, accordingly. I also saw a solitary man atop a distant mountain. He was a very old Sioux Holy Man, and he also saw me. We had climbed different mountains, but we had reached the same height. We therefore recognized something in each other. Later in life, I lived a while with that old Holy Man on Pine Ridge reservation, in South Dakota.

Now, at more than forty years of age, I still recognize events from that dream when I was a twelve-year-old boy.

When I came back into body, I was told that my illness had just turned for the better, and that I could go home the next day and rest there. I had been "gone" for several days.

When the voice returned, it said that six such voices would teach me, each in turn.

First, I must undertake the sacred *Fire Teachings.* These comprise knowledge of living a balanced and harmonious life in the manifest realm. Acquiring this, one would then reach out to touch the ethereal. This is called the *Red Road.*

The Fire Teachings took me four intensive years, starting from the day I had my dream. When I finished this learning, I felt whole, complete, perfectly balanced. I felt that nothing was lacking in me, and that if I lived this way I would always be at peace. My intention was to travel into the remaining wild areas of the North, and just live in harmony with the natural world. My teachers offered me an alternative.

My teachers said that I could choose to stay and continue learning. Since I did not feel anything lacking in me, I did not at first want to stay. However, it must have been fore-ordained as they had convincing reasons at the ready. They explained that I could begin the formalized learning of mystic ways. They explained it as the *Dreams of Stone.* These are the fundamental perceptions that we can reach as human beings. My teachers said that in order to being this path, I must set aside all the harmony and balance that I had acquired. I must begin over again.

They explained that the formal learning would take me ten years. Then, three-and-a-half additional years would be added to learn one particular consciousness. After this, a period like journeymanship would follow.

In one way or another, all my teachers said to me, "We are in the time of transition. Many old ways will go; many new ways will emerge. So there is a need to understand the foundation." That is what my learnings have been. That is what I have to share. The teachings are not always A to B, in some strict, logical progression. They jump around. That's life.

I want to present facts as simply as I can. I do not want to write to create any moods. I could easily write only from my Native self. This would then be another lucid-dream-symbols book. That does not cut it anymore. That is the moonlight realm. I hope to try to impart a little ray of starlight, distant sunlight, drawing nearer and nearer.

The formal search is for the rising sun of spiritual illumination, and is called the *Black Road.* The reason it is called the Black Road is not because its followers are evil, but rather because they dwell in spiritual darkness while seeking a higher light. It is a very, very painful struggle during which time no human comfort seems to reach our hearts. If we are content, we will seek no further.

During the fourteen-and-a-half years of formal learnings, I had nothing to do with ritual, sacred objects, chants, songs, or smudges. All the teachings were given purely in spirit, with only a physical fire for the enactment.

At the end of the ten-year learning, I arrived at the rising sun I had sought. I received my first eagle feather, symbolizing the ability to overlap manifest and ethereal realms. I also received my ceremony, knowledge of several strong medicine plants, and began to practice medicine ways. In the following years I traveled to the reservation of Uncle Mark, where I attended and eventually conducted ceremony.

The first person on the reservation (*rez*) to adopt me in the Native way was Marie. She said that I should be as a son to her, and she would be my mother. Later on, Helena also adopted me. It seemed only natural that Marie's father, the renowned Holy Man, Frank Fools Crow, should also take me as a grandson. We recognized each other. He was the old man on the other mountain.

When I was sixteen, I was given my spiritual name. My teachers said that it was who I would one day become, when these learnings were complete.

Chokecherry Gall Eagle

ONE

THE FIRE TEACHINGS ARE SACRED.
THEY WERE NEVER MEANT TO BE SECRET.

Light. Sparkling snowy reflections, dancing water ripples, soft and quiet moonlight, and raging fires.

The purpose of life is to generate Light. Light is awareness. The spark of life is the spark of Light.

Some of us are drawn to the soft, still moonlight. Others find peace in the sparkling, dazzling snowy reflections, or other manifestations. No matter which of the four natural Lights we are drawn to, we each are drawn to Light and warmth. As the sun illuminates our daily lives, so too, does the spiritual Light illuminate and warm us. While the cold moon reflects sunlight back to illumine our dark night dreams, we become a little more aware through our dreaming. Lighting comes briefly like a sudden and powerful revelation.

Only Fire is directly in touch with the surface of the Earth. The things that Fire represents are the way to achieve harmony with physical creation, and within ourselves. This is the Light generated through the physical realm.

Some people are drawn to the huge, leaping flames, while others prefer the warm glow of hot coals. This reflects our nature, or character. But we each have within us a Fire. It is composed of emotions, ego, passions.

Fire. The raging inferno, the dancing campfire, cuddled in love by the romantic fireplace, eating a meal cooked out of doors.

There is a custom that the men do the cooking from time to time. Today on reservations the men will make a fire somewhere near the house. They will cook the family's meal. It symbolizes that the Way of the Hunter, in touch with nature, nourishes the family and the whole people. It nourishes humankind to be in tune with the movements of nature, and to be at one with it.

As the young men cook and commune they sit in a circular pattern around the fire. This symbolizes the timeless continuity of life, and the renewable nature of creation. It also symbolizes renewal for the participants. We refresh ourselves in the company of others like ourselves. We share concerns, experiences, and our harmony with the earth and each other.

The Circle. The round base of the tipi, the shape of the sweatlodge dome, the Sundance lodge, the hole in the pipe—these are all circles.

The first part of the sacred Fire Teachings, as I received them, has to do with a physical fire in the center of a circle of white stones. This is all within the circle of people. The people are in turn within the great circle of the horizon points, marked by the Four Directions. And this is all within the continuity of eternity and the whole universe itself.

I came to know my main childhood teacher as Uncle Mark. He had me surround the fire with white stone, because Stone represents perceptions, or realities, or dreams. The stones are laid in a circle, symbolizing that this teaching is a something true for timeless eternity, and concerns harmony. The stones are white to symbolize the purification that comes with touching timeless harmonious spiritual realization.

Picture yourself alone, in deep wilderness. You are in the very heart of the wild, natural, and unspoiled world. There is no one else anywhere around.

Would this frighten you?

Imagine that you are alone in the wilderness, in the dark night. Do we not each sometimes fear the unknowns of the dark night? To be warmed, we have only to make a Fire. Then, we feel more secure, and start to refresh ourselves in some degree of well-being. The flames warm our body, and push back the dark night. Likewise, two lonely people kindle a fire of love to ease their isolations, and fears of the dark unknown.

Picture also that you are with a small group of people under these conditions in the wilderness. The fellowship of others helps to fire to seem brighter, and to push the dark night fears further back from you. It is the communing (harmony between peoples) that does this.

23

As you sit around the fire, cook a meal and share it, you laugh and tease. But, you give each other dignity. Then, you are sitting in a spiritual (mystical) circle. When someone pushes others aside to sit nearer the fire, that person is demonstrating that he or she will not willingly afford dignity to others. They demand ego-centered attention. We say that their inner fire is burning out of control. When someone sits further back than the rest of the circle, they are timid and afraid to share. They fear rejection, or to be proved unworthy in some way.

In both cases, fear is the motivation. It is a fear to be tested and proved unworthy in some manner. If you fear the dark night, the vast unknown, you might react by throwing more wood on your inner fires. You might react by turning inward, into yourself too far.

Therefore, I say that we must be willing to afford each other dignity; for only then can we live in dignity.

The first part of the Fire Teaching concerns harmony within the family group. It is the first intimate relationship among peoples. This can be the family that we belong with as a child. It may also be the family that we form as an adult.

Sharing concerns, assisting each other, a willingness to accept who the others really area, all this creates a harmony within the family group.

The warmth generated by this communal concern is an inner glow of satisfaction, contentment, and safety. This glow is Light being generated. It is the same Light as the eternal illumination of spiritual realization. This is how it reflects through the physical. Its range is like the physical fire. Some fires are small, and do not illuminate much of the night. Others are brighter, and push the dark night further away from us. Compared with the Light that shines through all of creation, firelight might seem small. Yet it is the only Light directly sitting on the earth, the only Light inherent to body levels. It is the only Light directly touching our mortal lives through body levels.

This is where we begin to learn about Light and harmony.

When I received the first part of the teaching, it was during a family cook-out over an open fire. It is the basis of ceremony that spiritual meaning and literal fact match perfectly.

During the cook-out, my teacher placed me into ceremonial consciousness and imparted realizations to me. In later years, coming to the rez (reservation), I realized that this was the ideal consciousness sought in Vision Quest. My teachers guided me to it frequently.

I saw the relationships of a fully functional family. I saw the sharing, laughter, concern, and love which generates a Light, through the warmth.

In the world, we associate darkness with aloneness. It is cold isolation. Light is associated with love, and harmony. Light eases the feelings of aloneness. It is a harmony. It is a song. It is a vibration that echoes other vibrations.

The roles of each family member may differ. One person might be the principal provider of material comforts. These may include housing, food, clothing, and other physical needs. Someone else in the family might provide spiritual comforts and be the rock around which the family gathers in troubled times. But the diversity of characters and personalities does not influence the harmony of the group, as long as each person is willing to afford dignity to the others.

As we grow and mature, we begin to develop friendships with those who more closely share our interests. While family may be concerned for you, they are not necessarily interested in those aspects of life which attract you. Thus, we find people of like mind with whom to share more fully our interests. We retain the base of harmony and warmth that we have learned through family; but we extend this ability to generate Light through friendships.

As we mature, we will have been nourished by this Light, warmth, and harmony. We will have become a more complete person.

As we grow in wholeness, we are really becoming balanced. The parts of being that come into balance are body, mind, heart. When we feel the kind warmth generated by family and true friends, when our bodies are developed and in calm readiness for whatever life offers, and when mind is clear and untainted by the imbalance of uncontrolled lusts, cravings, and ego-centered desire, then spiritual awareness may enter in.

This is the first part of the Fire Teaching.

When we have achieved this state of wholeness, balance, having it together, then we may become more spiritually aware in the manifest realm. Then we are generating Light. The first part of the Fire Teaching tells us that we must reach physical and emotional accord with others. It is physical or social harmony among peoples.

When we reach emotional harmony with others it generates warmth, and thus Light.

We must be straight with others, and honest. You cannot reach harmony if your relationship is based upon a lie. The first part of the teaching deals with striving to become more whole and complete through this warmth which generates Light from within.

The second part of the teaching deals with the change that comes to us when we are whole and complete. While the first teaching used a Summer Fire, set amidst the fullness of the earth and the fullness of physical sensations, the second teaching is a Winter Fire, set amidst the snows. This is the old-age consciousness of a clear mind after passions have died.

In the second teaching, the enactment was that I would choose a location, and simply build the Fire in the manner that appealed to me. Then, I was to sit in harmony and a relevation should come to me. Contrary to all of my previous experiences, my teachers would not be assisting me to reach ceremonial consciousness. I would have to get there myself. I was sixteen years old at this time.

It was a solitary experience. I simply walked off alone, and wandered until a place appealed to me. I chose the base of an old oak tree. It had once been burned in a grass fire. Much of its trunk was burned away and hollowed out. Yet it lived, and produced leaf and seed each year. Its enduring qualities were an inspiration to me. Here, I gathered the dead wood of Intent to make my physical, and inner Fire.

When we can calm the body, it should be perfectly resting and yet ready for action. We clear the mind of illusions, hopes, and wants. We feel the warmth of heart. Into this balance comes spiritual awareness.

I built a very small fire on the frozen, bare ground and sat close to it. As I approached ceremonial consciousness, I realized that my inner balance was reflecting to and from the natural world around me. I knew the one-ness within the flowing patterns of the natural world. It seemed that this flowing movement must be the Great Spirit in all things. Perhaps it is the breath of the Creator, the breath of God. I was not an observer, but fully realized my participation with the whole of creation.

It was November, and the cold ground was bare. As I reached different realizations, it suddenly began to snow furiously. Soon, the whole world seemed to be a white, swirling mass of harmony and one-ness. I walked out into the storm warmed by an inner feeling.

Reaching these perceptions, my perception of myself also changed. A lot of things can be seen in their true smallness when weighed against the standard of one-ness with the manifest world. The pettiness sometimes associated with purely physical existence can be erased here.

The teachings have been about warmth and harmony, so far. Now, we come to generating more Light. For, we really do generate Light.

We call ourselves Star Peoples. We speak of Star Knowledge. Like the sun, we can generate warmth and Light. Some people who follow a mystical path will even learn to drop material form and to fly through the manifest as a sphere of very beautiful Light. These are the little Star People. There is also the medicine man associated with the Star People. At one of the first ceremonial sweatlodges that I attended, six of these little stars came in. They were each about two inches across, and full three-dimensional spheres. They flew around the lodge, and the darkness was illumined. I could not think of a more beautiful sight.

I noticed that there seemed to be a song in the air. Yet, it was not audible to the ear. It was heard in the soul. It seemed to be their vibrations and their harmony with creation which caused the song. I realized that their song was their relationship to creation, both manifest and ethereal creation. Their different hues and colors blended to form a chord which resounded with all of creation as the sounding board.

Whether we generate Light as warmth with loved ones, or attain the ethereal form of sphere of Light, consciousness generates Light. The more aware and conscious that we are, the more Light we are generating. The sacred Fire Teachings set us firmly along this path.

In life, we pass through stages of learning the harmonies. The balance of the second Fire Teaching is usually attained quite naturally in old age. As the raging passions of the flesh have cooled, the mind is set free of distraction and illusion. It becomes clearer.

We feel the warmth, and want to share it with the younger generations. This is the kindly old grandparent that we might become. We each have within us this capacity. The Fire Teachings are the way to naturally understand, and perhaps speed up the process a little. When we have achieved the balance of the second teaching, we have touched the Great Spirit and wholeness of the earth. This touching merges the individual self with the whole. The individual self is thereafter changed. We can see the world as a whole thing, of which we are fully a part.

At this time, we might begin to exhibit spiritual ability. We might have seeings, or dreams. The seat of spiritual power is approached in this way.

For myself, this wholeness and completeness drew me towards wilderness. I resolved to walk northward, and to wander the last unspoiled lands. I would take such shelter as I found, and what food was given. If it would be my fate to be eaten by the wild creatures, then so be it. I would die within the flowing patterns of the whole, and even my death would be complete.

What I saw through touching the one-ness, is that upon dying, awareness opens and consciousness expands. The individual can see his, or her, relation to the Great Spirit, the Holy Spirit. If the person has over-emphasized ego and imbalance they will weigh themselves against this one-ness and find their reward accordingly. This does not mean that we have to be perfect people. We all make errors. It means the quality of heart, and your intentions. It is the spark of goodness within.

Certainly, we kill every day. We kill creatures to eat them, and kill plants to eat them. Through pollution we kill the rivers and the soil. We even harm the souls of our grandchildren through greedy acts. Yet, it is the spark of goodness that grows to perhaps illuminate our souls.

I have been with several people just as they were dying. I have seen how their consciousness expanded. Old Native people who are preparing to die say that they are "climbing the mountain." This means that they are going as far as one can in becoming aware of Spirit, and yet remaining a while in body.

The question that we ponder as mystics is, If we are going to die with expanded awareness and elevated consciousness, touching the Spirit in all things, should we not strive to live that way? And so, the mystic practices the art of dying, and of transcending.

As we acquire balance through the knowledge of the Fire Teachings, we might exhibit spiritual abilities. We may have prophetic dreams, intuitions, seeing, or be emphatic to a degree like the psychic ability of just knowing things. This is the Red Road that we talk about. This is the only Red Road. The Red Road is to live in harmony, wholeness, completeness, and a good heart. This leads to generating Light.

By its nature, the Red Road leads to discovering spiritual abilities. This is also the Bread of Teaching that Christ gave to the people. It is the symbolic bread that He divided amongst the many. I fully believe that He did this literally. But as His life was one long ceremony, it is also symbolic. The Word that He gave the people was also this bread of how to be nourished in body life by having a good heart, living with the Holy Spirit in all things. It is to generate Light through the Fire Teachings.

The wine that goes with the bread is the Holy Spirit and the ability to transcend earthly or mortal bounds. When Noah survived the flood, he planted grapes and made wine. Removing the clothing that represents custom and tradition, Noah sat naked in his tent. The tent symbolizes the reality that shelters us. Noah got drunk. He went beyond ordinary body awareness. He transcended.

One way to describe Lakota Vision Quest is to say that "they go beyond."

The twelve apostles asked Jesus why He taught the public in parable, and taught His close followers differently. He conferred the level of mystic on them, and then sent them out to teach, to heal, and to perform miracles. He also told them, that when a student has completed his or her learnings, the student will know as much as the teacher and be on the same level. Those who truly follow Jesus might do what He did. He caused the fig tree to wither instantly, healed the lame, and caused the blind to see. Jesus also taught his disciples to heal. The disciples said, "Be healed," and people were healed.

Can the communion of saints be much different than the total uniting of consciousness modern mystics speak of? Two separate people sharing one consciousness. Communing.

Christ knew what others thought. He knew what was to come. The error that many people make is to forget that He was also a fleshy man. He had a body, and emotions. One version of the Bible has Christ saying that He rose from the dead to show that not only are the saints holy, but that anyone born of woman can grow more holy.

He came to teach us how to do it. This is what is meant by taking up your cross and being His follower, to strive to grow more holy. On the reservations, an aspiring mystic can often be criticized. People ask, "Who do you think you are—Crazy Horse?"

Others try to diminish the aspiring mystic because they feel that they, themselves, are not following the path that they should. To justify their own lack of effort, they try to bring you down to prove that no one else can do it, either. Do not be sidetracked by them. They are lost to themselves and would take you with them if they could.

Likewise, many say that we cannot be like Christ. They say that He was the son of God. Yet, Jesus himself said that we can reach the same level when we complete our learnings. His disciples healed and taught. Jesus wanted us to follow His way actively, not as passive observers.

There is no such thing as a casual observer at ceremony. You are an active part of life, and cannot deny it. Even Albert Einstein, studying Light and the relationships between time and space, said that as you learn more about the universe, you cannot help but have a feeling like religiousness.

Of course, any mystic worth his or her salt knows that space is not rigid, but flexible. This depends upon the perception of time, or relativity. This is what interacts at every ceremony. One aspect of ceremony is that this fundament is embodied. I have been to sweatlodge where the whole lodge, a dome-shaped structure seven feet in diameter and four feet high, suddenly lit up inside. The lodge expanded in size so that a tall man could stand up and not be able to touch the ceiling. There are mystics all around the world who have transported (teleported) their bodies and objects over great distances. Some mystics can split consciousness in two parts. They drop the body awareness and fly as a free spirit. Some can leave their body in one place, and generate a solid body in another place. This has been particularly documented in India, but Native American mystics also do it. When traveling as a sphere of Light, you can generate this other body self. At the same time, far away in another place, is the original body self. This original body self can be talking and walking.

It is a difficult realization to deal with, and at first seems to contradict the idea of one whole self. Eventually, it gives rise to understanding more of the true nature of time, Spirit, and substance.

All this can begin with the Fire Teachings. It is about generating Light. We say that where modern society has gone wrong, is to artificially produce a cold and impersonal light to live by. This is symbolized by man-made lights. They, in turn, symbolize the idea that man can dominate or subjugate nature. You can use fire to light the night, and it is whole and complete. Harmony eases the dark aloneness of our mortal condition.

You can find warmth and Light through harmony with others, and with creation. The electric light symbolizes ego and domination—man against nature. There is nothing so sad as a solitary person in a large city, who feels lonely and turns on every electric light in the place, desperately trying to get warmed in their soul. The warmth comes from harmony with others, and society has made a cold and impersonal electric light to live by. Such light can never warm us.

The light that society lives by is man trying to separate himself from others, from nature, from eternity itself. It is flesh-oriented and ego-driven. That is a very cold and lonely light to try to live by. It is not natural, and like the electric light bulbs that symbolize it, has no warmth to offer us. I do not mean that we must throw out all the electric light bulbs, but the attitude they represent. It is the attitude, or reality that is wrong.

For those who argue, "If God did not want us to invent these things, and to use them as we see fit, why did He give us the intellect to figure them out?" The reply is that there is also the potential to commit sins.

The Biblical Original sin is not sex. Indeed, God told mankind to be fruitful and multiply. Mankind ate the symbolic fruit of the Tree at the Center, and gained knowledge of good and evil. Prior to that, mankind lived in the Holy Spirit, the Great Spirit in all things, and perceived only wholeness. All acts were natural, and within the Garden-of-Eden consciousness. This consciousness comes from being part of the whole, generating Light.

Within the movements of the whole, in touch with the Holy Spirit or Great Spirit, we still kill creatures to eat and survive. We pick plants to eat and survive. These acts are within the flow of the whole. We defend ourselves, and are still within the eternal circle of harmony with creation. There cannot even be a perception of a wrong act, if all of mankind lives this way. If you are balanced, you do not steal, rape, murder. If your consciousness is firmly established within the participation with the natural whole, you do not perceive that "sin" exists. To be able to commit wrong acts, you must remove yourself from this participation with the harmonious whole. You must be separated from the breath of the Creator, the Great Spirit in all things. You must perceive yourself as separate from others, separate from society, and separate from creation. You see yourself as an observer rather than an integral part of the whole. This is the knowledge of the tree at the center of the Garden. The Creator therefore said, "Let us deny humankind eternal life if they have knowledge of good and evil, so they are not as immortal gods."

The clue in Biblical accounts is that at first there was only the Creator. Darkness, unknowing covered the Void. When the Creator said, "Let there be Light!", it meant, Let there be Awareness. The desire to create it, became it!

According to the Bible, the sources of physical light—sun, moon, and stars—came later on. So the first Light was something other than physical light from a physical sun. And, the Light (awareness) was divided from Darkness (unknowing).

The Creator generated Light by His intention that it be so. And we are supposed to be made in His image. Another clue is that in the beginning, there was only the Creator. Out of the Creator's intentions to create, came all of manifestation and the spiritual realms. The Creator's intent, and awareness, became creation. Thus, we say that we can perceive the Spirit that is in all things. It unifies seemingly separate things into a coherent whole.

So I say that to dwell in darkness, or sin, is to be outside the harmonious flowing of the whole, the Great Spirit in all things, the Holy Spirit. It is to be outside the touch of God.

TWO

THE PURPOSE OF LIFE IS TO GENERATE LIGHT.
PART OF GENERATING LIGHT IS TO LIVE IN HARMONY.

When I was asked to undertake the ten-year path to learn the Dreams of Stone, or fundamental perceptions, I was told that in the cosmic scheme of things there is a place where the Fire Teachings fit. According to my teachers, learning the Stone Dreams would validate the Fire Teachings.

There are as many paths to generating Light as there are individual people. What I must speak about here is my path. My teachers assured me that the major teachings are something that we each have in common as human beings. I will be telling about very powerful and mysterious things. I am not meaning to impress you with my life. Rather, my hope is that you will be impressed with how magical and powerful life itself is. After all, I am just another man.

The events that I will describe form an overall pattern that took several decades of intensive struggle to unfold. Some events were months apart, some were years apart. This is the Black Road that I speak of.

The first notable event is the journey to void, a journey I took while living in Ontario. I centered my body, cleared mental activity, and felt my heart. This is how it works. Through inner silencing, you wish to go somewhere. You silently yearn, beyond mental thought-words. You can intend to go somewhere specific, but what happens once there is left open and free. If you have no specific place chosen to go, you will go where your spirit wills.

My intention was not to go specifically to the void. I wanted to get beyond manifest realms, and into deep space. I ended up in the void.

I felt myself being swept out of my body awareness, as when I was lying in the hospital bed as a boy. I found myself floating, in darkness, deep and empty. Sensations came and went, unbidden. There was no coherence to my awareness. I could not focus, but drifted, floating . . . aeons seemed to pass . . .

I seemed to be moving, but how fast, or through what, I could not tell. There was nothing to compare myself *to*, to indicate motion.

From far away, I sensed something approaching me; or I approached it. I saw spheres of Light of different colors. This was the first time I ever had seen them. I was told in my youth-vision that I would encounter these spheres of Light, and assumed they were symbolic.

They floated around me, and encouraged me to go with them. I seemed better able to focus. I suddenly perceived the earth, but it was a dim shadowy form. I perceived several historical events that formed a general pattern through our ages. When we reached my time, I could no longer perceive the earth.

Instead, I saw something that looked like the sun being eclipsed by the earth, or some other planet. It was like a corona of Light, with a round black disk blocking it from view. I tried to move past the planet to see the sun. It was the same view from every angle. The spheres told me to take this back with me. This meant that it is a medicine to ponder in the physical.

I came back to the manifest realm and found myself floating in the room above my body. My body was not in repose, or trance, or resting. It was talking and moving around, without "me."

I found it very unpleasant to have to go back into its limited confines again, after flying freely. But, I knew that I had to. When I settled into body again, I was suddenly aware in both "selves" of everything each had been doing. For several days, it seemed that part of me was numb, or in shock at this. I could not even begin to ponder it, or think about it at all. It took me several years before I could understand the experience.

My opinion of a concrete reality was shattered. In effect, I had been in two places at once. One of those places was the normal body realm, and the other was a visionary dream-place; but I was still aware on two different levels at once.

The medicine that I had been given to ponder was a sun eclipsed by a planet. The sun represents spiritual Light. The planet obscured the sun from all angles. Eventually, I concluded that manifest form, itself, blocks us from perceiving the spiritual Light in all its glory. While living in body states only, we do not directly perceive the Light. We see only the glimmerings of the corona. It seemed to me, then, that the thing that we must do is to break the chains that keep us rooted only in the manifest realm.

At the end of the first Fire Teaching, I saw the relationships between people and harmonious living. I observed the physical fire throughout these realizations as a twelve-year-old boy. I noticed the smoke. It rose upward and spread thinner and thinner, until it simply merged with the air. It got so stretched out that it disappeared from sight, though I could still smell it for some time. The point at which the smoke disappeared seemed to me like the dome of the heavens, an invisible barrier to the ethereal realms.

Where does the smoke really go, but to merge with the wafting breezes, the breath of God, Great Spirit in all things? Where does our mind go upon our death, but to merge with the Holy Spirit in all things, the harmony of the whole? Where does mind go when we die? Where does awareness go, and what does it encounter? I was led to ponder this through the first Fire Teaching when I was twelve.

Our being rooted in material form is what shelters us from having this knowledge barrage us daily. This prevents ethereal awareness from disrupting all physical activity. If we do not live in harmony and Light, cravings and physical enticements build further walls to keep out ethereal, or spiritual realizations.

This is the knowledge of the earth eclipsing the sun in the great void.

This does not mean that we must give up pleasures or sensations. It means that we can come to a consciousness where we rule passions and cravings, and they do not rule us. It means that we can transcend the limits of mortal form.

The next teaching did not come for several years. It has taken me many years to deal with the journey to void enough to carry on actively seeking. I did not fully understand until ten years were over. I was very concerned with the nature of time and space, as I seemed to be in two places at once.

Since my earliest memory, I recalled a life on the central plains. I knew what it was to be sheltered by a buffalo hide tipi, and what a great blessing it was that for the third year in a row there were no deaths or serious injury during the buffalo hunts.

Now, having found how to take these journeys, I decided to try to visit the location of that buffalo hunt. But I would do so in current times.

I regarded this journeying as a vision, or intense dream, and did not have any opinion about its absolute reality.

The journey began. I found myself standing on a small hill, overlooking the same flat valley. Large hills rolled away into the distance, and behind me to one side were familiar high hills that looked dark blue from a distance. The prairie grass was brown under a clear blue sky, and a small river bisected the valley. Across the flat, there was a gentle slope between the hills where hunters drove the buffalo down onto the flat. I recalled the roaring thunder of hooves ripping the earth as the herd was driven hard against the steep slopes of the hills. The hunters made their kills as they rode alongside the charging herd.

I half expected to see and hear the buffalo come down the slope once more, and grew sad. I knew that this was never to be again. I began to pray, and to *Send*

A *Voice*, demanding to know where the Buffalo Way had gone, and what would replace it for the People. The People need a way to live.

There was suddenly a very old, thin Native man beside me. He was dressed in modern clothes—jeans and plaid shirt. He identified himself by name and told where he lived when he was in body. I asked him where this valley was in the physical and he told me how to find it if I started from the village of Pine Ridge, South Dakota. I knew then that he was one of the six voices, and I addressed him as Grandfather.

I asked him what would replace the Buffalo Way, or if it could ever come back again.

He said that it would never return. But, he indicated for me to look at the black hills behind me. Though it was midday, there was a huge bright red sun about to set behind the hills. I began to watch it, fascinated. In my body life, I had never before actually watched an entire sunset. Something in me seemed to be absorbed by the red sun setting, and I somehow merged with it. I seemed emptied of something I had carried since birth, and the vacuity was being filled with something nameless. When the red sun had completely set, I turned and looked for Grandfather. He was gone. I pondered for a while how this sun could replace the Way of the Buffalo. Then I chose to return to the body realm.

Several weeks later, I had an intense urge to go to Algonquin Park in Ontario, Canada. There is a high granite cliff with a look-out point. I visited it late in the afternoon. In the body realm, there was a huge red sun setting over the high western hills that looked dark in the distance. The scene was similar to that in my journey. As I stared at the setting sun, completely fascinated by it, something seemed to absorbed me into it. I seemed emptied of my "self," and was filling up with something lighter, and more airy.

As the last trace of red set behind the hills, I turned and began to run as fast as I could down the narrow, slippery trail. It had rained earlier, and the steep descent was muddy. I ran full out, using short fast steps. A joy overtook me, then. Something poured out in that headlong run. I negotiated the rocks and tree roots, where one misstep could send me crashing head first over a cliff several hundred feet above the valley floor. I did not care in the least that one slip could easily cause my death. I poured myself out in the run, and began to feel myself filling up with something light, and airy. I realized as I ran, that I was being filled with the Spirit in all things.

If I died, the wolves could eat my body. What mattered, all that could matter, was to pour out participation with that endless Spirit in all things. I felt reborn in that run. When I reached the base of the high hill, I wanted to go back up and do it again. But I knew that such things come in their time, and cannot be forced.

In European writings, some have alluded to the teaching of the Red Sunset and have tried to make a mystery of it. There is no big secret, really. The sun is the light that we live by. The red sun is a fire sun of passion that we live under. It is the hot blood of physical living. For this red sun to have set upon our lives means that we have surpassed the *mortal condition*. We have certainly not become immortal. We can breach the barriers of mortal limitations. We can begin to sense, while in body awareness, what lies in the beyond. The beyond is what is beyond strictly body limitation. We are more in touch with the Spirit in all things.

This should replace the Buffalo Way, according to my teacher.

What was the Buffalo Way? Partly, it was co-operation and harmony between people. In order to live together, tribal or village hunts were arranged. By making such hunts, and sharing the bounty of the hunt, the village was given the means of material survival. Through the act of sharing, and harmonious co-operation, the village was given the means of spiritual survival. As individual buffalo merged with the whole herd to become something stronger than any individual, so too was consciousness and reality shared by the people to form a whole village, a tribal consciousness.

Rules governed the hunt and communal living. Severe penalities were given to offenders. Death or banishment was possible. Sent weaponless—and more importantly friendless—onto the vast prairie, one did not often survive.

With the liberation of the Red Sunset, you share because that is now your personal way, not because you have to. No penalities are needed; your nature is to co-operate and share. Yet, you do not give recklessly to those who purposely abuse your generosity.

At the end of the first Fire Teaching, I watched the smoke dissipate into the whole.

I realized that beyond this dome-like barrier lies the spiritual or ethereal realm. At the conclusion of the second teaching, I perceived that we, ourselves, can become aware of the Spirit in all things and weigh the purity of heart against this wholeness.

The teaching of the Red Sunset brings us to actively embrace the Spirit in all things, not merely to glimpse it.

It gradually becomes apparent that "realities" are but dreams that we have, or that we create. What makes one person into a lawyer, while another becomes a bricklayer, is twofold. It is partly inclination fostered by circumstances. Each person also lives within a slightly different world-view, and thus a slightly different view of self in relation to the world. This is the dream they are having. Because our world-views have so much in common, we can relate to others in our own society to some degree and get along. As one undertakes to learn ethereal matters, it becomes apparent that much more of our experience is but a "dream" that we are having. When I left my body and traveled around, it seemed to my free-flying spirit that *it* was real, and the inner core of consciousness. The first shock came when I returned to body and realized that I recalled a continuous sequence of events during the time my "inner core of awareness" was gone.

With the teaching of the Red Sunset, something that we dreamed was real is swept away, and a new realization of self comes instead.

After I had spent several years incorporating this teaching into my daily life, I was shown that I should move to Toronto, Ontario. I do not like large cities, but I had to be there for the next teaching. I found a co-operative house in which I had my own room and shared the rest of the house. Eventually, I found a job. In my prayers, I was being led toward surrendering more of the things that somehow define me as who I am. I found this terribly difficult to do, afraid as we all are that without these definitions of self "I" would somehow no longer be "me."

During my prayers and sitting in silence, I suddenly noticed that I was watching sea gulls swoop through the air in front of the factory across the street. But my face was turned away from the bay windows. When I turned around, the gulls were just as I had "seen." I felt that if this strange perception continued, this surrendering of self to Spirit would come. I did not feel ready at all for this.

I asked for a specific sign. Rarely do we ask for signs, and never do we demand that one particular sign comes as we wish it to be. But, I wanted everything to be absolutely clear that the sign was genuine, and there was no misunderstanding through meaningless coincidence. Though I knew only several people in a city of millions, I asked that an eagle feather be given to me within twenty-four hours. If this happened, I would know for sure it was the sign I sought, and no mistakes could happen. I would then trust, and let go of these parts of personality and ego-defined self.

The next morning, just after seven A.M., someone knocked at the front door. It was a man I had spoken to several times. He handed me something wrapped in newspaper. I opened it and found an eagle feather with the quill wrapped ceremonially in brain-tanned leather!

"You can make better use of it than me," he said.

"How did you know to give me a feather?" I asked in surprise.

"When you give feathers yourself, you will know that!"

"Where did *this* feather come from?"

"From a roadside eagle feather stand in Arizona."

"No, really."

"You can't ask that. Lessens the mystery," he smiled.

He seemed gravely concerned that this particular feather be treated respectfully. He said that he would like to return in Four Days, a sacred period of time.

I began to hold the feather while sitting in silent harmony in the Great Spirit. I felt myself looking two ways at once again. I did not know what this meant, but knew it was something very fundamental. Slowly, it seemed that I was taking the journey, but still fully in body! I had all the same perceptions and feelings as when taking a journey, but while in body. I reached a place where it seemed I could go no further, or perhaps would go no further through some inner choice.

I began to pray intensely, to breach this barrier to mortal perceptions. A voice spoke to me, saying in pure Light, "Move ahead, the way is cleared." Something in me seemed to burst open, and my awareness seemed to soar.

A calm settled over me, a nothingness. I heard wingbeats that were not audible to the ear. Somehow, I "heard" them. My eyes popped open wide and I gasped for breath as something slammed into my chest. Each side of my chest was caught in a vise-like grip, tugging at me and trying to lift me upwards, higher and higher. I let go, and was lifted.

I suddenly knew that a Spirit Eagle had gripped my chest in its talons, and was lifting me. I discovered in later years that this is the mystical Sundance upon which the annual ceremony of the plains is based.

My eyes were open, and I was looking out the bay window at the tree tops and sky beyond. A point of golden-yellow Light appeared in the sky, and grew at a tremendous rate. It quickly filled the sky and touched all of creation. The very air seemed to be a golden-yellow substance. I was a golden-yellow Light substance. My breathing seemed to be the inhalations and exhalations of creation itself, of the Great Spirit. My body seemed to be a dream that I was having, my life seemed a dream I once had.

I wished to know where in creation I was. The reply was immediate. I instantly saw the room from a different perspective. I was looking at the place where I had just been sitting. My body seemed to just instantly be across the room. I had no time for surprise, because I was suddenly looking from another perspective. And another, and another. Then I was back where I started. I felt great peace and contentment, and did not understand with intellect; but this transporting around the room explained everything to me. I was content, serene. I felt like I was floating in the void, yet was also in body. Rather than being in two "realms" at once, I had become aware of two realms touching through the golden-yellow Light.

In later days, I came to understand that my body seemed to be transported to each of the four directions, regarding the center from each direction. I sat at the center.

At the center, which lies mid-point between the manifest and ethereal realms, is the golden-yellow Light of spiritual illumination. It is the rising sun I had sought for ten years, almost to the very day.

The Light filled the world, and filled me. But, though I had found the rising sun, I still did not truly know where it came from or what caused it to be.

In the next four days of holding the feather while sitting in silence, I received my ceremony, knowledge of several important herbs, and other gifts of Spirit. I began to see some events to come and sat all day with the feather. This was too important to worry about material things. I lost my job. I could not pay my rent, and eventually had to trade my services as a laborer for back rent. I had no more money for food, and for days I did not eat.

But before that happened, the man who had brought me the feather returned on the fourth day. He asked several specific questions, and I realized that he had not yet reached this level. I told him several of the things that I had seen in the visions of the future, but did not answer his questions. I realized that what transpires to the seer is private. He had not come to me for help with a problem, he just seemed nosy and wanted to hear what happened with the feather. It seemed to me that he was delegated to bring the feather, but was curious about the whole thing.

It was soon after this time that I began to visit the reservation of Uncle Mark. I knew that I should receive the next teaching there. However, two elderly men objected to my complexion being a little too pale for their personal taste and did everything they could to block me. Being raised without such concerns, I was an innocent to their manipulations. When it became clear that the next teaching was just not going to happen, I was rather at a loss. Now what?

If we are to learn, a way will be found.

One evening, back in Ontario, I became aware of a strange man talking to me over a distance. He said that he was sitting in a mid-winter ceremony, and told me exactly where this was. He said that a medicine woman present had a vision that this man speaking should hold a very particular ceremony for my benefit. Certain teaching tales would be told, and ceremony would be held. It would be in several weeks at the house of a mutual friend on a different reservation. Having learned the hard way to be skeptical, I asked if this mutual friend was also at mid-winter ceremony. When I was informed that he was, I asked that he be told to telephone me the next morning and invite me physically.

Early the next morning, my friend called to invite me and I began to prepare for the teaching. Before I left for my friend's reservation and the ceremony, I made my own ceremony.

The ceremony at my friend's house was attended by about twenty people. I knew no one but my friend and his family. When the altar was made, and the

Sacred Pipe filled, the teaching tales were told. I knew they described what I was about to experience. The drum was brought in, and songs would be sung to invite the Spirits to dance with us. It was a Ghost Dance.

With the steady heart-beat of the drum filling our ears and hearts, the rising and falling cadence of the songs filling our minds, people rose to dance with the Spirits. I sat in silence, and prayed.

The drum and singing eventually faded to nothing, and all I could hear was the wing-beats of the Spirit Eagle! It circled the room once, and slammed into my chest. My eyes popped open in shock and I gasped for air as the talons dug into my chest, tugging to lift me bodily. I hesitated and fought, but suddenly saw something before me that allayed my fears. I let go, and was lifted.

I saw the whole house spinning upwards to the level of the clouds, and then the house dropped back to earth. I floated slowly, drifting over the Great Lakes, and then across the Canadian plains. Drifting, slowly turning southward to the sacred Black Hills, heart of the Turtle Island called North America. Above the central mountain, I floated and rested.

Winter faded, spring passed, and still I floated. Lamenting and yearning reached me, and I floated over the Teaching Mountain. Many Native people were fasting for guidance. I smiled, happy at their earnestness.

I heard a very old man asking to use the Great Powers one last time. He explained that it was not to glorify himself, but to demonstrate to the people that such things still exist.

I noticed that the world below me was bathed in the golden-yellow Light. Good, I thought. Finally I can turn and see where it comes from. Turning to look above myself, I saw only the darkness of deep space. I realized then, I am the Light.

I returned to the house where my body was. I entered to hear once more the singing and the beat of drum. I still perceived the golden-yellow Light, but when I entered the body I still seemed to be floating. I was looking down at everyone from the height of the ceiling. I made my body settle to the floor. When I touched it the drum and singing stopped.

The next morning, the helpers teased me that perhaps all the medicine people should learn to meditate so they can levitate, too. This happens in Yuwipi ceremony.

Yuwipi ceremony is to call in the Spirits. They can come as spirit creatures, or the spheres of Light. The man that conducts the ceremony is tied hand and foot, wrapped in a star quilt, and this is also bound tightly. When the tights are turned back on after the ceremony, the man has been untied by the Spirits. Some men have been found at this time to be floating bodily up at the ceiling. However, not all that try this today get untied, let alone float.

The significance of finding the source of the spiritual Light cannot be easily grasped from body states alone. It is the journey to the lodge of the sun, of which the teaching tales speak. It is one of the piercings of the realms of being. It certainly does not make us "as gods." It is the relevation of our own spiritual being and the ability to generate Light. This does not contradict any religion. It is like higher self. Buddha said that when you see the earth with the eyes of the sun, you begin to understand.

It was after this that I discovered that we ourselves might fly as spheres of light. The hues of that Light represent the qualities of our medicine and path. Since I had "gone to the center," I encountered the meaning of symbols. The colors of the spheres represent the type of awareness the person had.

In my youth vision atop the mountain, I was told about the spheres of Light, but did not see them. At that time, I assumed that they were symbolic of something. I was to learn that they are very real. Six of them came into sweatlodge. They were each about two inches across, the fully three-dimensional spheres. They were very beautiful to see as they flew around the lodge, singing.

Some time after the teaching of the sun shining on the earth, the friend whose house was used approached me for guidance. I had him stay overnight, and we smoked the Pipe together. Later, I prayed in seclusion. I saw what he would dream, and asked at the time for guidance for myself, to understand more of what was happening to me. Then, perhaps I could help others better.

I found myself at my sweatlodge (new life badge) floating as a free spirit. I looked it over, and saw that everything was fine. It was in an area owned by the provincial conservation authority, so hikers might one day wander by. But it was in a corner not easily accessible. One had to climb a hundred-foot cliff, or walk a mile from the road to get to it. I decided to go see what Grandfather was up to.

Then I found myself at Fools Crow's place in South Dakota. I had visited him several times a year, camping on the prairie behind his house. Now, I was looking in from above the house as though the roof was transparent. He was saying that this night he would hold ceremony, but first he was going to use the Great Powers for the people to understand that they still existed. I determined to stay.

I wandered around the rez, checking on friends. I saw a friend at the evening powwow, with a young Japanese man. The Japanese man said he wanted to use the pay phone and as he walked into the hallway he passed a clock that read 8:30. I followed, and in the hall four young men were about to jump on him and knife him because one lost an uncle in Vietnam. To them, Oriental was close enough for revenge.

I went back to my friend and whispered in his ear to go help his friend in the hallway. I then went back to Fools Crow's place, where the ceremony was about to begin. I floated in the room, watching. I knew that about a hundred feet away, in a tipi, sat my body. I ignored it, it did not understand yet, and would only be confused.

During the ceremony, a young boy began to stare at me, and he was deeply wondering. I decided to sit next to him. It seemed as though my body suddenly materialized just behind him, and I edged forward into the circle. He smiled as he made room for me. When the ceremony was done, and everyone stood to stretch,

I simply returned to where my body was lying in bed. Before entering it, I wondered how I appeared when I flew as spirit. I saw myself as a sphere of Light, and saw also the colors I generated. Then I entered body, and was awake in body. I was early morning.

When my friend awoke, he told me his dream and it was as I had seen it would be.

About six months later, when I was visiting Fools Crow, my Lakota friend arrived with a young Japanese man. My body began to tremble, then to shake. This was the journey I had taken.

I tried to control the shaking. When I tried to split some wood for a cook fire, I nearly chopped off my own foot, and had to stop and go off alone.

Fools Crow attended a function held at the nearby Native college, and when he sang and prayed great raging thunder-clouds came racing in. They filled half the sky in an arc, and sat there against the breeze, motionless. Hour after hour, they barraged the earth with sheets of roaring orange lightning. People were afraid, but knew that the Great Powers still exist. My body periodically shook violently.

My friend invited me to go to powwow with them that evening. I looked him in the eye and said, "If you plan to be around your friend at 8:30, I will not go, but if you plan to wander off anywhere, I'll go." He looked at me strangely, but said nothing. Being Lakota, he is used to mysterious things.

When they returned later on, they said that at 8:30 four guys tried to jump the Japanese man, but a voice had whispered in my friend's ear and he helped him in time.

My friend looked intently into my eyes, to see if I would say anything, but I was silent. As soon as they left, my body shook again. I sat in a borrowed tipi, though several people had asked me to come into the ceremony.

After the ceremony, a young boy was the first to come out of the house. He came straight to the tipi and sat down.

"You were here the whole time, weren't you?" he asked.

"Yes."

"And yet you sat next to me in the ceremony?"

"Yes, but don't tell!"

As far as I know, he never said anything. Later on, I gave him a treasured hunting knife that I had kept for nineteen years. His mother said that she would bead the scabbard and he would dance with it.

I knew that if I attended the ceremony that day, my spirit would be there. My body shook from the sure knowledge that there really is another "me," and that it was in the same physical time and place. This was too real, too immediate. My mind just could not bend to encompass this Stone Teaching. Obviously, some sort of time projection was also involved; it was not just me traveling around in my own time. In the Far East, they say there are cases of mystics being bodily in two places at once. This must be how it is done there as well.

This cast a fresh light of understanding on previous experiences. When I had traveled to the buffalo plain, the old man who said he was my teacher was real. I somehow knew that, but the impact now hit me fully. It was in the place where the manifest and ethereal meet that I talked to the old man, attended Fools Crow's ceremony, and I flew as a sphere of Light. It was truly *real*.

I have spoken to people from different nations, or tribes. A Mohawk woman told me that as a young girl she saw the spheres almost nightly. She said that people generally knew that these were Spirits, or living mystics checking on things. She also recalled that Christian teachers said that this was evil witchcraft. As a consequence, the next generation began to fear the old ways, and mystic spirituality.

When you pray, you sometimes see flashes of light. We say that someone is just looking in. When the spheres come, they are three dimensional and of very pure light. At the Teaching Mountain, they have been frequently seen.

I spent several summers camping with my wife on a lonely part of a rez in the Dakotas. Across from our camp, a quarter mile away, was a river. Beyond that, another quarter mile, was a buffalo jump. It is a very high cliff that forms a sheer drop from the surrounding higher prairie. In the old days, hunters would stampede some of the buffalo off the cliff to provide meat, clothing, and shelter.

Almost every night we watched the spheres for hours. They flew up and down the cliff, and along the river. There was one place on the flats they seemed to favor; and we eventually learned this was where the people camped when they had a buffalo drive.

I was wondering where to make a sweatlodge, and would have liked to be near the river, though the water was alkaline. One night, I dreamed of a lodge sitting on the bare prairie, and dozens of Spirits were going into it. I built my lodge there. When it was time to mark the outline of where to plant the poles, I saw a perfect circle laid out in the grass, and a smaller perfect circle where the stone pit should be. The entry way was marked as well.

All these things are about generating Light. We might even drop body and fly as a sphere of Light, ourselves. This is star knowledge. We are the Star People.

Star People are individuals from any race or religious foundation who learn to generate Light through their transcendences. Nations may know about star knowledge, but individuals are Star People who recognize each other through the Light they generate.

THREE

RED AND BLACK, THE TWO ROADS ARE THE SAME.
THEY ARRIVE AT THE SAME TRUTH, TWO DIFFERENT
WAYS.

The two types of path that I talk about are generally for two types of people. The Red Road is what most people follow. It is the way of growing in harmony, until in old age we acquire the wisdom and spirituality of a Grandfather. In this way, we grow in Light and harmony and cultivate spiritual abilities. These might include lucid or prophetic dreams, seeings, and ceremony.

The formalized Black Road is that of the mystic practitioner, or so-called medicine man. Really, we each are people of medicine, but some are called upon to demonstrate greater us of the same powers. This is the thing; it is all the same Power.

It is the inherent ability to generate Light, and to live in harmony! Before I begin to explain symbols, I have to say some things. Medicines are an *understanding*. Certain symbols carry meaning. It is easy to get too deeply involved in the meaning of symbols. It is too easy to forget that the important thing is the ability to dream of the symbols at all.

Dreams are in the realm of the moon. We can do many things in dream.

We can even help or harm others in dream.

Dreams are but a reflection of the power of living in sunlight, spiritual awareness. The moon generates no light of its own. It merely reflects sunlight back to us through the dark realm of sleep, and unknowingness.

The sunlight reality is to take journeys beyond flesh. The moonlight reality is to but dream that you took a journey. At first, it might seem that our dreams comprise ceremonial events. "Ceremony" is a consciousness. Ideally, we should be able to just enter that fundamental consciousness when we choose. But, we are not living ideally. So, ceremony seems to be the reality where cosmic meaning and literal fact match perfectly. That is to say, the objects and ritual used evoke the meanings they inherently embody. So when you perform the rituals in the time-tested way, the desired result must come.

There is no sense in trying to Sundance unless you first know how to properly attend sweatlodge ceremony. It is like trying to win the Grand Prix with a soapbox car you nailed together one night in your garage.

Until the time when I asked for and received an eagle feather, I used no object. Yet, the consciousness that I shared with my teachers was ceremonial.

Certainly, mystics around the world have ceremony and ritual. In every Way it is known that we eventually surpass the need of ritual and objects. Jesus taught His way of mysticism to the apostles, and seemed not to use ritual at all. He usually just healed.

Some people have greatly misunderstood the Black Road. It is a long period of emotional seclusion wherein the practitioner concentrates on mystic revelations. That is all. Some people have said to me that they sometimes fall off the Red Road, onto the Black one. They mean they lost their way for a while. They seem to think the Black Road is an evil thing, but it is not.

The Black Road is:

the journey through spiritual darkness
while seeking the higher Light.

It is the path of the mystic seeking enlightenment. No one makes an arbitrary choice to walk the Black Road. It is not a career move. You do not choose it, you are chosen for it.

Red and Black, the two roads are the same thing: seeking harmony and Light. How the two paths get there, is different. On the Black Road, you wander the cosmos in search of the rising sun. On the Red Road, you step out of your tipi, and look up. It is the same truth, arrived at two different ways. I want to point out something. When you acquire and live in the harmony of the second Fire Teaching, all of your acts will be in accord with Great Spirit, the Spirit in all things, the Holy Spirit Breath of God. This is a degree of Holiness. Lakota (Sioux) say *Wakan*. This is two words. *Kan* means something like pure ethereal being, spiritual being, other-worldly. *Wa* means something like the quality of being able to do something, or achieve something with an object, idea, or manifest thing. Together, they more literally mean, "can do something with ethereal nature," but *Wakan* is usually translated as meaning "Holy." When someone is becoming very spiritually aware, the people might begin to refer to him (or her) as a *Wakan* person, a *Wicasa Wakan*.

The same truth applies to all levels. We participate with the Spirit in all things, which is really like the Creator reflected through creation. We are also an integral part of this whole. One truth, on different levels of awareness and understanding.

Symbolism is as old as creation. There is a consciousness where symbolic value and literal reality match perfectly. This is what I call ceremonial consciousness. You do not need objects to ritual to enter this state. Once you know the consciousness you can begin to try to stabilize your entry into it. The purpose of the time-tested rituals and ceremonials is to help us acquire the *feeling* of this consciousness. Particular songs serve the same purpose. When a buffalo-medicine-man sings for healing, it is very different than when a grizzly-man sings for healing. Yet both sing for healing. The particular tone, or hue, or consciousness flavors the *mood*. The two consciousnesses entered are not unlike each other in basic substance. The different medicine ways of the singers give the mood, hue, and feeling. If these two men each would fly as spheres of Light one day, they would generate different colors and hues of Light. Yet, they would each generate a *pure Light*.

When you conduct ceremony, a similar consciousness change comes. Yet during one man's ceremony you hear Spirit Eagles crying out and feel the wind as they beat their wings near you. In another man's ceremony you hear Grandfather Buffalo come in with four stately but earth-shaking thudding steps.

One basic similarity is that ethereal things are perceived. The one conducting the ceremony probably received his powers (each of which is control of an aspect of consciousness) during a Vision Quest. Everyone in the ceremony perceives the Spirits coming, because they really do come, and really exist. The ceremony opens you to better perceive ethereal reality. This gives rise to ritual and ceremonial objects. One man might be given a Pipe to use, and so he always uses it. If others try to copy his Pipe, or ritual, they can be harmed, or harm those attending. They do not have the vision that empowers the ceremony.

Some ceremonies are more generally used. The basics of the different ceremonies are the same, but individuals can have particular medicines they use. This individualizes the ceremony.

I have already mentioned the symbolism of Fire. Everything in creation has symbolic, or cosmic meaning. The source of understanding meaning, and symbols, is the golden-yellow Light of the center. Meanings become clear in the moment of illumination. All meanings become clear for an instant. Gradually, these meanings filter down into body states and slowly make body reality a more spiritual thing. Meanings become incorporated into daily living as we become more adept at reaching spiritual awareness. We can slowly begin to interpret dreams and visions. Not every Pipe Keeper or medicine man can interpret symbols accurately.

Not only can this be applied to Native American symbols, but also to Biblical symbols. To explain meaning, I will indicate a direction which one can follow on one's own.

All of the creatures, plants, weathers, and natural phenomena have symbolic meanings. The spiritual (medicine) name is revealed. It is not intellectually thought up. It is based on who and what that baby will one day become. The Holy Man prays, or even fasts, and the name is revealed. Until then, he knows nothing about that little baby to be named. He might see the spiritual path the child will one day take, and some of the accomplishments that will be life achievements. From this, the name is revealed. He might just know that this person is to be named "Crazy Wolf," meaning "acting differently," not insane. That the baby will one day have a vision of wolf-teachers, and follow this medicine way, is then revealed.

Non-natives often ask for an Indian name. A lot do not even know the right way to ask, but their ego wants a name, and to belong. They often get a social teasing name. Natives get this as well. But Natives have the spiritual name of great meaning also. One white man came from Austria and wanted an Indian name. He did not follow a sacred path and was not in the Native fundamental earth awareness. Everyone knew that he liked to travel around the world a lot, so he was named in an Indian langauge, "white man who likes to travel around a lot." He thought it sounded just fine in the Native language and practised saying it. We say our own sacred names rarely, perhaps in prayer.

In older times, each person had their own name because they had their own path through life, and things to achieve. You might have someone named Red Dog, who was the son of Two Bears, son of Thunder Watching. Each person had their own name which described their spiritual character, medicines, and cosmic role in the scheme of things. Both a public and private name could be given.

The direction I want your attention to turn is this: Dreams and symbols can be interpreted because they reflect back to us a hint of the sunlight reality where meaning and fact match perfectly. I call this state ceremonial consciousness.

Everything comes back to the center. Everything flows out from the center. The Pipe ceremony involves gesturing to each direction, and offering smoke. In addition to the four cardinal directions, we might include "that which is above us" and "that which is below us."

The one offering the Pipe is, of course, at the center of these.

The sweatlodge is round, like the horizon. The entrance faces east, whence comes the light of day, and warmth. It signifies revelations of Light. For those who walk the formalized Black Road, the entrance faces west, whence gathers the darkness awaiting dawn's illuminations.

The tipi is round at the base. It signifies the horizon and the eternal circle. The Sundance lodge is also round. On Vision Quest, one makes a circle to fast within, or marks the directions in some way. In all these cases, we are within the circle of the horizon, and thus also the directions, and we are standing at the center of all we see. We are at the center of this eternal renewal.

At ceremonial functions, there can be softened soil. When the sweatlodge is made, a shallow pit is dug to hold the white-hot stones. The soil from this pit is softened up, and the stones and twigs and roots are removed. This is "mellowed earth," softened and ready to receive a seed. It symbolizes that before entering spiritual undertakings we are to make ourselves also like mellow earth, ready to receive the seed of spiritual awareness, and Light to grow within us.

At the sweats, the soil is made into a mound three or four feet before the entrance of the lodge, between the lodge and the fire that heats the stones. In the tipi, there could be mellowed earth just west of the fire, between the principal man of the lodge and the fire. This was usually in a square or rectangular shape. This is also at Sundance. The shape signifies the unused earth forces and something called *Skan* (pronounced sh-kan).

Medicine people can draw upon this unused power or energy. It is a refreshing energy that helps purify us.

Confusions can enter in when you ask someone for guidance. If you ask a good person, who is rather holy, that person will suggest what you should do. In the Native social ways, it might even seem that he or she is commanding you, but this is a suggestion. Everyone has free choice, and you can choose to ignore their advice and go elsewhere.

If someone says that you must have certain things to be in accord with their medicines, perhaps it will make you feel uncomfortable. Then do not do it. Perhaps you do not belong in accord with that person's medicines.

Also, when you ask someone for guidance, or spiritual help, they cannot ask you for money, or even hint for gifts. This is spiritual law. Spiritual power is given to help others, and one cannot make a condition of that help to be any personal gain.

Some people can put a thought into your head. You suddenly just want to buy them a washing machine, or pay or fix their car. Wait at least four days and see if it was really *your* idea. With discernment you can tell. To do this intentionally is an abuse of spiritual ability, bad medicine.

When you seek advice, guidance, or healing, the only thing you give is a little bit of tobacco. It you require healing from illness or bad medicine, the Holy One might ask you to bring certain things inherent to the ritual, such as some cloth of the four colors, and perhaps to bring a little bit of food for the feast afterward. But many could bring food, for a potluck dinner.

Someone in great and urgent need sometimes sends a Pipe or an eagle feather to a Holy One for help, particularly if they are too ill to travel to see him personally. If you have a good experience, and afterward feel like showing gratitude, you might get a blanket for the old man so he survives the winter more easily. Perhaps you want to get him a bag of groceries. That is also fine. Most of the Holy Men give these things away later on to poorer people.

You should not feel offended if a Holy Man later on gives away the present that you gave him. He had the pleasure of receiving it once; you had the happiness of giving it. The Holy Man wants someone else to have the joy of receiving the blanket, or gun, or whatever you gave him.

When Grandpa Fools Crow invited me to stay with him, we finally reached consensus on how that would work. Since I had several things to accomplish, I believed that people would assume that he helped me to do them if I was living with him. So I said I would rather wait until I achieved these things, and no one would get confused about it. Shortly after I attended his ceremony in spiritual form, he asked me again and I accepted. Since he asked me to come live with him, he also said that I would live with him right in the house, and that he would support me. In the past some had come to ask if they could camp on the nearby prairie and once in a while come to the house to talk with him. Those who did this supported themselves.

Grandpa treated me as any member of the family, and even bought me cigarettes once in a while. He went out of his way to buy me good quality used clothing and shoes, and a nice black hat. The food that I ate was partly offset by being added to the list of his dependents for the monthly food allotment, called commodities. At the time, each person was given enough food for about a week and a half of eating. The canned meat was of such poor quality that most cans of dog food looked better. The tins of lard we were given to cook with only added to the problems of white-flour noodles and white sugar we received. The powdered eggs were mostly eatable, but the cheese was full of coloring and chemicals. Yet, it is survival.

On the rez, people joke when they have a fat middle, that they have a *common bod*, a commodity body.

It is a good idea to be careful about which gifts you accept, or keep. Sometimes a gift is given and you begin to have dreams. There is the potential that the gift is the vehicle through which someone bad wishes to influence you. Gradually, you find yourself doing things you might otherwise not have considered. You begin to feel a blind loyalty to the gift giver, and then you are their *dog*.

It takes discernment to judge this. It happens all around the world.

In the end, each person is on their own, unique path. You do not borrow symbols from others. You do not copy ceremony. You will hear people say that they follow an old man's medicine. They might even say that they are under his medicine. This is not necessarily a good thing. In general, true spiritual people merely point you in the right way so that you can follow your path. Each person has their own path through life. We walk over the face of the earth. Some will cross rivers, some will climb mountains. Some will wander the dry places. We have the sky and weathers in common, loneliness, the human mortal condition. But, each walk is unique. You can ask others how to climb mountains, but you still have to do it to really know what it is like and what is up there. Your particular climb will be different than anyone else's. Where others go right, you might go left.

Likewise, in medicine, someone teaches you for a little while. You go onward with this new knowledge. The experiences are yours, alone. For this reason, Native philosophy is one of non-intervention. You let someone struggle through their obstacles because it will test them and make them stronger. On your walk, you will encounter both good and evil people. In my dream-vision, I saw people in different places. Some became instant deep relatives, family for life and beyond. Others were enemies who wanted me dead. On your walk, you might meet the trickster. He can look like a little boy, a young woman, or an old man. It is someone who seems good, but is really evil and out to harm you. It can be anyone. This is the subject of the false-face masks.

The masks looks like a happy, smiling face. You like to see it when a dancer wears it. When they dance near you they trip a string and the mask swings open in two parts. This reveals the ugly evil face hidden behind the smiling one.

So when you ask someone for help, or guidance, they can offer advice that even sounds like a command. You have free choice to accept or reject their advice.

Listen to your inner feelings. Reach in to your clear center. It is not the voice of reason, but gut-level intuition. Live the harmony of the Fire Teachings and you will hear this inner voice more clearly.

I have dreamed about many objects: pipes, rattles, drums. I have not done anything about them. They are dream symbols. Some people rush right out and try to make the objects in the physical realm. I know of one young man who saw someone use a lance in a dream. It wasn't even his own lance. So he tried to make one in the manifest, and he got seriously hurt.

Many people get caught up in objects, ritual, and customs. The important things happen in clear ways. When the world fills with golden-yellow Light, you are fully in body and also in the ethereal, it is real. When you climb a mountain to pray, and eagles fly circles around you screaming out in joy, it is real.

When you go to sleep and dream about eagles, it is symbolic.

When you try to journey somewhere and then interact with people, it can be real. Those people recall interacting with you. I have had conversations with people in this way, and in body those other people recalled the whole talk. Just because you talk to someone in the Indian way, does not mean they are a good person.

I was once sent to establish whether a certain couple were corrupt in their conduct with Spirit. I came as a faster, seeking visions. They offered to guide me. I should have been the one to ask them to guide me. They did not even come close to proper spiritual behavior and could hardly wait to get me into their ceremony. I can appear very unkowledgeable about Spirit when I choose to do so; they saw nothing in me to be alarmed about.

In the sweat they tried to get me to smoke my Pipe with them, though it was already sealed for the fast. The man wanted an excuse to refill it with his own things. I played dumb, and stubborn. They wanted me to sing my personal medicine songs "so the spirits will recognize you are the one to help." That is such bullshit I almost laughed out loud. If the Spirits can't find you they are pretty dumb spirits.

When the man later took me up the mountain, he did not stop to rest the ceremonial three times. He just stopped any time he wanted, about nine times. At the place I chose, he asked me where my altar should go. If he was any good, he would have known. So I told him the direction of my altar, and he put it at the wrong place and refused to move it. Then, he produced a bunch of things he said his wife made as offerings to the spirits. They were awful things, full of bad medicine. I knew this was going to be a fun fasting. He turned to go, and I asked him if he was going to sing the sacred song to make the circle around me. He was not even going to do that. He said to watch all around, something would come to guide me soon.

I looked around the fasting circle, and remained unaffected. I held my "show" Pipe, one elaborately carved with my medicines on it. It didn't matter. Back in my tent was my original medicine Pipe sealed in the sacred way, and I was really fasting under it. They could do anything they wanted, it would not touch me.

Soon, there was a deer standing nearby. It was in the open, and I should have seen it approach. It had just suddenly appeared. I pointed the stem of the Pipe at it, and, demanded that it tell me its name, or identify itself as being of the light. It refused. I told it that therefore it must cease to help that couple and do only things or be returned instantly and forever to void.

It shook its head violently toward the couple and snorted at them. Then, it looked at me once, and was gone forever.

A novice would have thought they were being blessed by the appearance of the deer. I picked up my things, and left the circle.

The couple asked why I was back early and I did not even bother to answer them. They asked if the deer came to me. When I said that it did, they smiled broadly, beaming. Then, I said that it shook its head and snorted at them. They were in shock; they had lost their spirit helper.

Such things go on sometimes all around the world. We are supposed to use our own way. The ones who abuse power are not everywhere, but you only need to meet one to be in serious trouble. I did not receive my ceremony until I had been learning for sixteen years. And then it came at the hand of six medicine men, each a master of one medicine way.

The ceremony may have seemed long in coming, but it is *my* ceremony.

There are ceremonial songs. I have never tried to learn them. In sweatlodge, I prayed the whole time. If I wanted to sing, I reached out in consciousness and communed with the man conducting ceremony. Some were shocked when I did this, they knew right way. But I knew the songs as well as they did. We shared one consciousness. No one refused when they felt what I was doing, because they also felt what I was all about and knew that. When I began to conduct sweatlodge myself, I could suddenly sing the songs as well as my own personal song. Eventually, my experiences took me to a place where I felt the song of the Star Peoples inside me. From this, a song came. It has no words, but vocables.

But, for thirty-six years I had no song. I did not rely upon songs to change consciousness. The song is to help us acquire the consciousness. It is a mood, a feeling. It is better to acquire the consciousness than to know all the songs on earth. The songs are a help along this way, the objects can be a help.

A canoe can be a great help in crossing that last river before entering the great deserts. When you have crossed the river, you need not drag the canoe across the desert with you. It has served its purpose, let it go. Look ahead. Keep walking. New wonders await you.

So, I was going to tell you about symbols. But there is a lot to clear up. The realm of dream belongs to the moon. The light from the moon is but a reflection of the sunlight hidden from us by the position of the earth. The moon has no light of its own. Dreams have no awakening of their own. They reflect back to us, through symbols, some hint of sunlight reality. Sunlight reality would be that when you are out somewhere praying, an eagle lands right beside you and you have a telepathic talk. Reality would be that a rattlesnake curls up by you while you smoke your Pipe, and then calmly slithers away when you are done.

Dreams are to go to sleep and see things. This is symbolic.

Sunlight reality is that when a child is dying, a Holy One prays and the child is happy and playing in just moments.

Moonlight would be to have everyone picture the color blue while someone waves crystals and other objects over someone to re-align their energy.

There is some indirect sunlight reflected through that somehow. It is like weak moonlight compared to bright sunlight. Some people prefer to follow moonlight in the hope that it leads us to the rising sun. I do not believe that it does.

FOUR

THE BASIS OF ALL NATIVE CEREMONIES.
IS THE FOUR DIRECTIONS.
YOU ARE AT THE CENTER OF THESE.

The North stands for wisdom and clear-mindedness. It is like the kind old Grandparent who has wisdom born of experience. He has gone beyond the pull of raging passions. He sees things clearly from this vantage point. In symbology, the North is the place of snow and pines. It can be peaceful, renewing energy. It is also the cold, severe wind that cleanses the earth of disease and germs.

The East is where the sun comes up, led by the Morning Star. It is the warmth and light, causing things to grow. It also symbolizes mystic revelations of Light.

The South is the place of lush growth on earth. It is warmth through the immediacy of physical nature. It is the fullness of body experience.

The West is where the sun sets, where the red sun sets. It is the gathering darkness through which we await the rising of spiritual illumination which helps us to see further and live in warmth and Light. It is the dreams and visions that guide us through the darkness toward Light.

You can read much about the directions in many other writings. The important thing is that they relate to us. These are aids at arriving at the center. That is what they are really all about.

The thing to keep in mind is to arrive at, and always return to, the center. Through the use of the directions we are really doing the same thing as in the Fire Teachings. The levels of the Fire Teaching deal with four parts of self. Body, mind and heart are taught within the first teaching. Arriving at spiritual awareness is the second teaching. I was only taught two teachings, covering the four levels of self, yet it took four years for me to learn.

These four parts of self correspond to the directions. When we have arrived at body centering and have inner balance, when mind is cleared, and when heart is filled with warmth, then we perceive Spirit. Through the use of the directions, we are stirring to do the same thing. We are trying to align or balance these aspects of self.

Every ritual object that you use to mark the directions, or in ritual itself, narrows the field of perception. The more objects are used, the more the field of perception and awareness is narrowed.

It is better to just align the parts of self. This is what the old wise ones do. In my times with Grandpa Fools Crow, I saw him use elaborate ceremony. I also saw him merely light a store-bought cigarette and gesture the directions with minute flickings of his wrist. He used both ways, as circumstance demanded or as people needed.

The Pipe itself was given to the People by an ethereal woman, White Buffalo Calf Woman. When she left, the Pipe remained manifest. It was a particular Pipe for the whole nation. This was a special Pipe. She said that she would be back. It has also been prophesied that one day the Pipe would no longer be needed.

The Pipe usually has a wooden stem. The simple ones usually are the powerful working Pipes. Elaborately carved ones are show Pipes, almost like a badge of honor someone has. The show Pipe might be brought out before the People sometimes, but the simple plain one is used for ceremony.

The wooden stem of the Pipe stands for all growing things. Sometimes an eagle feather is hung where the stem and bowl meet, to symbolize the center and the mystical eagle feather of this knowledge. The bowl is often red soapstone, catlinite, named after a white artist who once painted it at the quarry. Followers of the formalized Black Road sometimes prefer black soapstone, traded from the Canadian Rockies. Today, there is a road that goes right to one place it is found.

Stone represents perceptions, hues of consciousness, medicine dreams. The stone bowl means this, of course. There are countless things that can be attached or carved on a Pipe. Each would symbolize a particular thing, and narrow the field of perception to that one medicine. If your vision decrees it, you might follow that one field of perception toward attainment.

The important parts of Pipe ceremony are gesturing the directions and the symbology of the smoke.

The smoke is said to represent our prayers, lifting upwards toward the ethereal. What the ethereal woman really advised is this:

Make your breath visible.
Pray with a visible breath.

The ethereal meaning is this:

When is your breath visible?
It is visible amidst the frosty snows.

It really means that to get answers to your prayers, you should pray with the clear purifying energy which is represented by the frosty snows of the North. This energy is sometimes called *Skan* (sh-kan) or *Taku Skan Skan*. Skan means something like divine substance in movement, and is sometimes alluded to as the wind. It is something moving, always moving, but only through itself and yet touching all of creation. It is a cleansing energy.

It is like when you have used up a lot of energy and it is very late at night. You shiver and shudder as something almost electric races through your body. This is like Skan.

Sometimes you are intent upon what you are doing. Suddenly, you get startled.

Something peculiar might be happening. All the hair on the back of your neck stands up. This is like Skan.

It is an energy. The first times that you feel it, it can seem like a jolt to the mind. It clears all mental activity for a few seconds, and we are not used to that. The first time I traveled to Uncle Mark's rez, I was wracked by wave after wave of this energy for three days of driving. It was to prepare me.

Long ago, the ethereal woman said to use this energy. Then our prayers would travel fleetly to the spirit realms.

I believe she meant this energy, and many others have told me they also understand it this way. The whole usage of the Pipe is meant to help us align the parts of self, and if we then use this energy once we are balanced, our prayers will be heard.

Since I was taught fundamental perceptions, I look for the root beneath the symbol. This is what I am telling you about. The entry into the golden-yellow Light is the fundamental perception underlying Sundance. The ceremony of Sundance is the enactment of the mystical event. I heard the rush of air that can be said to be the wings of the ethereal Eagle. I felt pain in my chest as the levels were pierced, which my mind says is the Eagle piercing me. The sensations were very real, and intense. How I describe the cause of the sensations is personal. A mystic from the Far East would say something else, because he would perceive a different cause, or hue, of the same experience. To me, it was an ethereal Eagle.

In the modern Sundance ceremony, the chest is pierced physically, symbolizing this piercing of the veil between realms. Slim cherry sticks or buffalo bone splints are pushed under the flesh of the chest and you are strung to the sacred tree in the center of the dance circle with a long chord. Once tied to the tree, you dance and eventually rip free. The tree is rooted in the soils, embedded in manifest life. When you rip free, you are signifying that you are ripping free of being rooted solely in the physical. Then, you are not governed by only manifest perception. It is sometimes said that when you pierce four times, you are a medicine person.

The ethereal meaning of this is that if you pierce through the four levels of self, you are becoming holy. Also, only men pierce. Women undergo piercing each month, with their cycle of the moon.

However, if you have not learned balance, and if you have not prepared properly through learning sweatlodge fundaments, you will not, indeed can not, get any benefit from Sundance.

The tree is rooted in the soils of manifestation. So are we. Trees are even called the Standing People. They reach upwards and outwards with their branches, striving for light and the living water that falls from the skies. When we break free, and rip the twigs and the bits of flesh from our chests, we are breaking free of our mortal condition. Then, we are to be uplifted as on the wings of a great eagle bearing us to the ethereal.

When you Sundance, it will be sunny. If thunderclouds come and stay a little ways off, rumbling, the Thunderbeings are checking to make sure all has been done properly. You can tell when it is an ordinary thunderstorm and when spiritual awareness permeates the acts of the clouds. If it rains on the dance circle, or if lighting strikes anything to do with the ceremony, even the woodpile for sweats, it is sure that something is gravely wrong. If the ceremony is done properly, it will be hot and sunny, always. That is part of the ceremony.

The participants in a Sundance rise well before dawn for ceremonial sweatlodge. Before first light, they are prepared to greet the rising sun. This symbolism is all taken from the mystical rising sun of spiritual illumination. The sacred songs are sung by drum groups in turn, and you dance in a circle around the sacred tree. You will get very little break during the day, and you will dance right through into dark night. This symbolizes the Black Road of seeking the rising sun. You will have no food or water for four days. In these fundaments are not followed, it is not a *real* Sundance but something imitating one. It says something about those running the ceremony. If you are properly prepared, you dance right through and at the end of the ceremony you feel full of energy, revitalized. Some people are not prepared and collapse.

No matter what else is in Sundance, it is an enactment of a person's arrival at the golden-yellow Light of the center between the realms. We even wear two eagle feathers above the head, each symbolizing one realm. One is on the right side of the head and the other on the left. We hope that after the ceremony these two realms have become as one. The center is where the Light is actually perceived. We are then elevated beyond the limits of our mortal condition. Because I was taught the fundament, I look for the intrinsic truth when I dance at the ceremony. I believe that it is better to try to experience the fundamental perception.

Native ways and some non-native ways lead to the same place. The Native way of North America is rather slow, but quite sure if you properly follow the purifications. The shortest period of time to begin to understand these things is thirty years. Not everyone pursues these matters vigorously, and so they take forty, sixty, seventy years. Ceremony is like a safeguard while learning. We begin to feel certain hues of consciousness in safe or controlled conditions with the parameters set. In some non-native ways one can progress more quickly, but they are much more difficult and some are not quite as safe. Christian mysticism can be understood in about twenty years, but is arduous.

As Christianity has been passed along, some parts of the teachings have been over-emphasized while others have been ignored. The big question that people ask about Christianity is, How does one get to be like the apostles and use spiritual power? I will discuss that a little later on.

There are symbols at the heart of matters. Which kind of Pipe you have, and take to Sundance, is much less important than your inner state and readiness. Likewise, there are whole systems that teach these understandings without the use of any things. You should recall the Native ways are a *system of development*. There are other systems. There are indigenous, or Natives peoples, all around the world. In all Native ways, there is a grain of fundament underlying the system. This tiny grain of Light, like a seed of pure consciousness, is what we eventually see, and experience, and hope to grow within ourselves.

Long before I ever received a Pipe, I conducted Vision Quest for others and prayed for people who were ill. When I received a long-stemmed Pipe, Uncle Mark said, "See what it is about for seven years; begin to set it aside then."

I have already mentioned the truth of the Pipe. Everything comes back to consciousness. Consciousness and perception are represented by Stone. The so-called medicine wheels, stone altars, are embodiment of hues of consciousness. You must be able to have experienced the mystical center before entering one to pray. You must be an aged and illuminated master before ever trying to be a helper gathering the stones for one, let alone construct one on your own. Until you have reached that level, you would only be assembling your illusions.

Likewise, at buffalo runs leading to jumps, where the herd is driven over a cliff, stone lines sweep out in a "V" shape from the jump. Some non-natives speculate that the stones were used to prop up branches to act like a fence to keep the buffalo running the right way. Actually, Stone is the important thing. It is not a visible thing. The old man making medicine for the jump, extends awareness to include the stone lines. The buffalo cannot cross this medicine line once driven or lured into the right area. An old man from Alberta told me this. He was a power man himself. His grandfather taught him this.

There are also symbols at Vision Quest. There are different ways to fast. Some people fast within a circle of tobacco that they sprinkle on the ground. Some fast within a circle of tobacco offerings tied in tiny pouches, called *tobacco ties*. A few fast within a circle of stones. It is their particular path to do so. It symbolizes that they have learned fundamental consciousness, and are sheltered by this learning. Their visions are usually in this regard. The important thing is not which kind of stone is used, or even that stone is used at all. The important thing is to arrive at fundamental consciousness. To fast within a circle of stones, you must have already experienced fundamental consciousness. If someone guides you, they must have experienced different fundamental consciousness. They must be a Dreamer of Stone.

The first time, or times, that you reach such a perception, the *content* of the experience can distract you from understanding the *nature* of the experience.

As an example, perhaps a hawk circles overhead, crying out as you pray with the Pipe. It lands right by you, and you have a telepathic talk with the Spirits through it. The fact that it was a hawk will stick in your mind. You will want to get hawk feathers or talons to put with your medicine things. What was said through the hawk is more important than the fact that it was a hawk at all. The message is more significant than the messenger. But even more important than the message is that you reach the consciousness where this can take place at all.

You do not realize the changes to perception, and the mood and feelings that went along with it, or what this means. With numerous experiences, you begin to notice how the perception of time was altered, and also space relations. It was the fact that you changed consciousness and had an experience at all that is significant. The content of the experience can guide us toward further experiences.

A large portion of the earth is water. A large portion of our bodies is water, about the same proportion. A large portion of our consciousness is fluid and flowing.

The soils of the earth are actually a quite thin layer. Upon this, everything depends and grows. Likewise, this is the portion of our complete being that is experiencing the fullness of physical sensation and reality.

The bulk of the earth is Stone. The majority of our total being is consciousness and perception. The gutrock that holds together, and supports the whole earth, is Stone. The gutrock that holds together and supports our existence is consciousness and perception. On the level of physical reality, perception is how we define ourselves in relation to society and to the physical world. Through this, we build self-definition, personality, character. This is partly what makes one man become a lawyer, while one woman becomes a human resources officer for a global company. They each live within their realities.

One person becomes a sheet-metal worker, while another is a hunting guide in the Far North. As people grow more aware, they discover that they can actually change their realities by first changing their feelings. Reality is partly a feeling about ourselves and the world, and partly also our associations of relative definition.

Relative definition is how we describe or define ourselves in relation to other people, circumstances in our life, and how we see ourselves in relation to the manifest world itself. We know ourselves, for example, to be our father's son or mother's daughter. How others behave toward us reinforces our ideas of self, role in family, and in the world. Likewise, a career is a large part of self-definition. But even beyond that, body and its apparent limitations are a definition we *allow* to restrict our experiences. By firmly believing we cannot get out of body, and believing in the rigid solidity of substance, we keep ourselves confined. We have defined our total being in relation to body limit in the physical.

Our perception of ourselves is likened to a dream. When we actually take a journey beyond body, it might seem that we had a vivid dream. But it is an actual experience. In my own case, I could recognize this because my body level kept walking and talking. To my freed consciousness, floating in the room watching body talk and walk, manifest life itself seemed like just a dream it was having.

Each is a valid perception, and in its own way, a reality.

The question of the nature of time arises. If my body-self kept on walking and talking, and yet my spirit-self witnessed events unfolding over years, then what is time, but a perception? Certainly we notice that time as measured by a clock does not accord with our personal sense of time. Sometimes two hours drag by, and other times they fly by.

This is dependent upon our relative definition of self and the circumstances we encounter. It is associated with changing consciousness, so perception also changes.

To enter the perception of eternity, or timeless spiritual awareness, is to change fundamental levels of consciousness. This begin with changing our *feelings* or having them changed by circumstance.

Albert Einstein noted the relation between time and space. It is a relationship where the changing of one must affect the other. When your perception of time changes, so too must your perception of space (substance) change. That is to say, when you can visually perceive that the sky is a vast dome beyond which lies the ethereal, your sense of mortal, or measured time changes. You might then perceive or sense the timelessness of spiritual awareness.

When you are not actually perceiving the dome of the heavens, but see instead that space reaches out forever, you have a different perception of time. One perception is linear and the other is circular.

In ceremony, this effect is noted. Practitioners do not bother with pseudo-scientific explanations.

The effect comes when things are done right. One can enter a sweatlodge and experience this. The lodge is a dome-shaped structure about seven feet in diameter and four feet high. During ceremony, a tall man can sometimes stand up and not touch the roof. This is because, as one is brought into a different fundamental consciousness and perception of time, space is literally altered.

The Shaking Tent is this way. The tent is about four feet high and three feet across, like an upright cylinder. Yet inside, during ceremony, a man can stretch out and not touch the walls.

The power used is called by different names. The experience is real. It is a matter of consciousness, and very real fundamental perceptions. Likewise, we confine ourselves by keeping consciousness limited to body outlines and solidity. Yet, when your body disappears in one place, and appears somewhere else instantly, solidity is suddenly just a vague idea you once had.

I have met an old man who did this, and once actually saw a middle-aged man appear. He was suddenly just there, looking around. He realized what he had done, and laughed as he did a little dance. When he saw me, he sobered up quickly. He was surprised that I had seen this clearly.

If you are living in purely body levels, even if you witness this, your brain takes over and demands a logical explanation.

If you have had mystical experiences, and fundamental perceptions, then you have the necessary quickness of awareness to perceive accurately what has happened. As we pray, or enter silent one-ness, it seems that we enter a slower perception of time. We grow more calm and serene. The perception of time beings to approach spiritual awareness. We think that we are slowing down inside.

I believe the contrary is true.

Stone represents consciousness and perception. As we heat the rocks for sweatlodge ceremony, the atoms in the Stone begin to move all around. They speed up their activity. This slowly causes the rock to glow red, and then white hot. Most of the Earth is Stone. They say the inner core is molten lava. Symbolically, what I believe we are doing is actually speeding up more and more, raising the vibration, and thus consciousness changes. As consciousness speeds up and perception is altered, we perceive spiritual time and the Light. With this, perception of space must be altered naturally.

As we grow more accelerated, we approach the speed at which the golden-yellow Light vibrates; and when we match its speed of vibrations, we perceive it. Certainly, it is all a matter of consciousness. The center can also be described as the consciousness where a certain relation between time and space exists.

This is one way to look at it.

The reason that a particular person conducts ceremony is that he has had these experiences. By entering these perceptions and changing consciousness, he gives us the opportunity to feel what it is like. Also, his spiritual ability helps us with illness. Perhaps it is the memory of changing consciousness that guides us to do it ourselves, one day. Rather than call it changing consciousness, or hues of consciousness, it is said that someone uses a certain power. The change of consciousness is accompanied by a change of perception. Perhaps a buffalo, or an eagle comes into the lodge. We do not even say that it was a spirit buffalo, just that a buffalo came in. The Spirits that come in can act upon us physically, for good or bad. So we know them to be real in some way, and we show respect.

It is merely taken for granted that changes to perception happen in ceremony. That is what ceremony is. So it is not even spoken of. Rather, the particular content is sometimes spoken of because it indicates the hue of consciousness, the medicine way someones uses. It might be said of someone, "He uses badger medicine." This will imply a whole range of meanings. The spheres of Light also imply a whole range of meanings. They are each Light being generated from awareness. They are different colors, and hues. These imply meanings. The ability to manifest as a sphere of Light reflects the qualities of awareness.

Certainly, Jesus also transfigured into pure Light atop the mountain.

It is unfortunate that this has not been understood. Jesus told his apostles that when they were done learning, they should be on the same level as their teacher. This would include generating Light.

The disciples did travel around teaching and healing. Whether any reached transfiguration is not clearly told in the Bible.

All of these things concerning consciousness and perception are in the Bible. They have been misunderstood or de-emphasized for centuries. Very little is made of the fact that Jesus was almost constantly going off alone into natural areas to pray and commune. This is so akin to Vision Quest fasting that the connections should be plain.

What is apparently lacking in the Christian way is the learned mystic who guides others along. Yet Jesus said that the student who finishes his studies will be on the same level as his teacher. The error of Christianity in my view is to say that by dying, Jesus somehow took away our sins. If so, why is there still evil and sin in the world? Many ask this question.

Jesus taught how we can grow more enlightened and spiritually aware, ourselves. We still have to do it. He showed us how.

Jesus' life was like one long ceremony. The acts that He did, embody meaning. He caused the lame to walk. He caused those incapable of following their path to get up and do it. He caused the diseased to be healed, and caused our wrong thinking and attitudes to be purified of the diseases society teaches us as truths. He even rose from the dead, to show the eternal nature of spiritual existence and mastery over the material realm.

It is said that the person who overcomes the earth (manifest limitations) is given a white stone (purified perception of harmony) and a white robe (spiritual ability through harmony and purity of Light-awareness).

You see, earth symbols are pretty universal in meaning. In this way, Stone and Fire can mean the same things to people of any culture as they purify mind. Individuals can understand at different levels, because we all grow at our own rates and in our own direction.

Centering is often described as living in the ever-renewing moment of the here and now. Another way to say the same thing is the consciousness of the "i am." This is also the center.

> *whatever exists, is me.*
> *that which is, so i am.*
> *i am that which exists.*
> *i am that am.*
> *i am eternal.*
> *i am eternity.*
> *i am that am.*

FIVE

LIVING "FOR" THE MOMENT IS NOT THE SAME AS LIVING "IN" THE MOMENT OF HERE AND NOW.

One can seek understandings personally and directly. One can also emulate the attained ones. By trying to duplicate the effects of their elevated consciousness, students hope to elevate their own. This is the basic principle of many Ways. In this manner, the sage who has transcended might describe the attributes of his new-found awareness to students. After certain realizations, he finds that the deep sense of a personal past becomes less important. The future is not yet here. So the sage does not string together many single moments into a progression. Rather, he accepts each single moment as a whole thing in itself, not necessarily leading anywhere else but into itself.

When you live the consciousness of centering, you are in the moment of here and now. So, students try to live in the here and now to gain centering. It is a reciprocal relationship. The consciousness has attributes. By trying to live the attributes, we hope to gain the consciousness. The sage accepts each moment for what it holds, and lives that moment fully.

The public teachings of Christ, if followed, would lead one to the Light and harmony of the Fire Teachings. One would arrive at the old-time good-heart medicine of Native peoples. In older times, having a good (strong) heart was crucial to Native life. People of bad heart were seen as imbalanced.

The private teachings of Jesus, given to the apostles, lead us to being practitioners of spirit ways.

To Native people, the ability to react instantly to changing circumstances is a mark of achievement in consciousness. Another mark of achievement is to be able to give a spontaneous talk in a detailed and clear manner. When an old man gets up to talk, it should flow directly from his spiritual awareness. Speeches are not planned, but flow.

Centering is somewhat like the calm amidst the swirling flow. The flow is comprised of time, water, wind, manifestation, or thought. It is like the calm point around which life itself swirls and eddies. To stand fully centered, one is standing symbolically on strong, natural Stone.

When you are centered, you are still in the manifest. So one event follows another. These moments are not linked in any absolute way. You can change your feelings and actions to respond to each moment. The true warrior, living centered, can go from idyllic peacefulness to total battle consciousness from one moment to the next. The inner core of consciousness, being realized and apprehended, gives the sense of touching timelessness to some degree. Centering is so named not only because it is the center of the manifest circle. It is the center between manifest and ethereal realms.

The declaration, "i am," is a simple statement of fact.

In body states, this declaration is sometimes expressed wrongfully as *I* am. This is over-emphasis of the ego-defined self. At its varying levels, the consciousness of centering is that the individual self, the "i," has blended to some degree with the vast subjective realm of pure Spirit, represented by the "am."

When we travel to void, we leave behind character, personality, and all relative definitions of self. Stripped of ego and its ramifications, we perceive ourselves to be a nameless existence, something that is aware. There is no longer any "I" around which awareness can focus. For this reason, I say that the ethereal void can be called pure subjective awareness. Objective awareness is the part of us isolated from pure spirit by the safeguards of mortal limitations. When we transcend this mortal limitation, we can set aside ego and embrace a full realization of ourselves as both physical and ethereal beings. This realization of our dual nature is the realization of centering. It is sometimes called the real, or true self. It can be a time of knowing, "i am that which exists" through touching the one-ness of all things.

The grand consciousness that embraces all of creation can more often be felt on a smaller scale. The very same truth and consciousness comes. It's just that the scope of the realization encompasses more, or less. It the same Light.

When we enter ceremonial sweatlodge, we are advised that we should pray very hard, and then we will not get burned. The harder you pray, the less the intense steam and heat will affect you. The more that you place consciousness and perception toward the ethereal, the more that you are elevated above the physical body heats and passions that can burn you up in their all-consuming embrace.

It can be in sweatlodge that you are sitting above the ground, levitating. When you reach down as far as you can, you cannot touch the hard-packed ground under you. In such cases you have been symbolically and physically elevated above the material realm.

The harder we pray the less we are consumed by the heats and intense passions of life. We can still enjoy them fully. We do not get uncontrollably consumed by them. They do not rule us.

Some people are not prepared for ceremonial sweatlodge. They do not understand centering or mellow earth, and they are in danger of passing out. This also sometimes happens at Pipe ceremony. It is not the heat and steam of the sweatlodge that make people pass out; it is the change of consciousness that they are not used to. The first time I attended sweatlodge I wondered how the others could gasp in the steamy air and sing so loudly. I discovered that the preparations for ceremonial sweatlodge begin in the moment you decide to attend.

To become like mellow earth of the altar is to bring body to the balance of physical centering, to clear the mind of daily events and distractions, and to feel the warmth of pure heart willing to face the Creator. Into this mellow-earth self the seed of spiritual awareness can be planted, and grow.

All of the ceremonial things used are symbolic of changes to your consciousness and perception. When you live in the proper conditions, you just live right. You live in accord with universal, or cosmic harmony. If someone is in need, you help them. When you are in need, you will be helped.

I once was hitchhiking and wanted to get somewhere by nightfall. I had a large backpack and my wife also had one. We even had our dog with us, hitchhiking. It was impossible to get a ride, so we prayed about it. A man in a compact car stopped, and we squeezed in. He drove us over two hours out of his way to help us out. We had no money to give him for gas, but he even bought us coffee.

In ceremonial consciousness, you stop having unreal expectations arising from ego desires. Ego is in its place as a minor definer of personal self. It should not be dominant. Perhaps ego would tell you that you need a house to spend the night in. It might be that to learn something you need to sleep in the woods, under the stars, on a frosty night. So, very often ego should be made to just be quiet a while. Let us accept life as it is, not as ego thinks it should be.

Prayer works. You must learn to pray in the right way. If you are Christian, meditate on the Lord's Prayer. You can soon realize that it is a very good thing. It says the Creator is Father of us all, *our* Father. Our Father is in the ethereal, who art in heaven.

When I pray, I look skyward and say,

Grandfather.

Christians say,

Our Father.

The prayer is the same, the hue of consciousness is different. The Lord's Prayer places your perception toward the ethereal. You think about what lies beyond the dome of the heavens.

Our Father, who art in heaven, hallowed is your name . . .
Grandfather, Wakan Tanka . . .

Christians say to fear God. I say respect the Creator.
When I pray in Lakota, I say,

Tunkashila,
Grandfather, pity us, pity me!

In both prayer ways, we recognize the Creator by a family term, Father, or Grandfather. And the Creator can act through creation. Christians say, "As it is in Heaven, so it is on earth."

And so we pray with respect, because the Creator is divinity. We say, "Make every step a prayer, every breath a prayer." Make every breath a participation with the whole, the Spirit in all things, Holy Spirit. Christians seeks the state of grace.

We are each a full part of creation. We touch the earth as all creatures do. We eat and reproduce. We should enjoy the weathers, live at the center, be content.

When we participate with nature, you kill only what you truly need. Some of the old people say, "If you killed it, eat it." If you feel your full participation with the whole, you must realize that the same Spirit touches all things. This naturally includes the animals you prey upon. You feel a kinship to them. To kill without need would seem like murder. Living in harmony with the land is not just living *off* the land, but to live *in* the land. You do not survey landscape, you are an integral part of the landscape.

If you can realize within yourself that "i am all this whole," to wantonly kill creatures and plants would be like cutting off your own foot. All the good teachings are attributes of living in a centered manner.

Rarely is the fullest declaration of "i am that am" made. The declaration can be made by a mystic who has transcended. It is the deepest mystical center, and he who has transcended at that time has no name, family, history, country, character, personality, or ego. For this reason, I sometimes write the word "I" in lower case "i" to indicate the transcendence or lack of ego and personality.

All that exists is a presence that fills creation through full participation with the Spirit in all things.

I was taught in the Native way called talking over distance. You call it telepathy. It is also emphathic, for feelings also carry knowledge. When I was young, though I had not met my teachers in the flesh at that time, I learned that they were flesh and blood men alive at that time. Several of my teachers died before I went to their rez.

It might have been easier for me to cope if I could believe they were Spirits. But then, I would never have dared to think I could one day be like them. I would have thought, like most, "Well, Spirits can do these things, and I am only a mortal man."

A mere human being does not feel he has to try to be like an ethereal being. Yet, we are each partly manifest and partly ethereal ourselves.

If someone transcends, and realizes their full participation with the one-ness of all things, they have the authority to direct that whole. On other levels, centering is the same declaration of one-ness.

SIX

THE BASIS FOR USING POWER IS CENTERING AND BALANCE.

This basis is found when one completes the Fire Teachings. It is also found, if that is your path, at the golden-yellow Light of the mystical center. These are the same truths, along two paths.

I quickly discovered that there is one power with many hues. There is one power, reflected different ways.

I was shown how to find what a plant is used for. You silence the mind, balance the body, and feel your heart. Then you silently wonder without mental activity.

I was shown how to put someone into a fasting circle. You center your body in balance, clear the mind, feel your heart, and through the silence you pray.

It is all centering. When you enter the mid-point between manifest and ethereal realms, almost anything you wish can be so. However, there are cosmic laws about what you can really do. If you wish wrong things, or to profit, or to harm others, you will be paid back. If not in this life, then in the after-body realms you will get what you deserve.

I know of one Pipe Carrier who started charging for sweatlodge. He also began to let women enter the lodge on their moon (monthly cycle). It is not a matter of cleanliness, but this is a woman's piercing time and she is full of power then. For several years, if this man tried to conduct ceremony, he got ill and began to vomit violently. That was his pay-back.

The shuddering waves of energy clear out the mental activity. This helps us achieve the proper state from which to pray.

If you touch the Spirit in all things, you begin to recognize what lies within that flowing wholeness, and what is an interruption to the flow.

My friend the grizzly-dreamer once said he heard there is a sacred song that, if you sing it, you can find out what any plant is good for. I do not know any actual song for this. There could be one. I know there is a harmony you can enter, and any song would be based upon this hue of consciousness. The song would be to help you reach the consciousness.

The sacred songs have different melodies and words. The Calling-the-Spirits songs are different than Pipe songs. At the heart of each is the consciousness of centering. The tone and words of a song help to direct your awareness to a particular perception.

Though you enter the same centering to use powers, it can feel different to split a thunderstorm than to ask for healing. Splitting a thunderstorm is something some people do. They divide the storm into two parts, so part goes right, and part goes left, missing camp. The camp is in the middle, and dry. It symbolizes that the man has divided his consciousness into two separate parts. He stands in the middle, or center. Grandpa Fools Crow reputedly did this, though I did not have the chance to see it. There are also people who can be in two places at once.

When we first travel to the center, we carry with us any preconceived ideas and beliefs we might have. Lacking purification, we notice the content more than the nature of the experience.

To clearly understand, we must return to the center having purified awareness. Perhaps an eagle lands beside you and you talk with it telepathically. The kind of creature that you talk with has some significance. The creature is a messenger of the Grandfathers. The creature is not originating the talk. The conversation is carried out through the creature. You are talking to a Spirit, or a mystic somewhere else.

The creatures have some significance. We say the coyotes are used to carry messages. If you are in the body realm you sometimes hear them singing and understand in your own language what they are saying. If you are Lakota (Sioux), you hear them in Lakota. If you are Cheyenne, you hear them in Cheyenne. If you are German, you can hear them in German. The communication is pure, and your mind translates it into your own language. When I talked over distance to my adopted mother Marie, she heard me in Lakota. I was speaking English. I heard her in English, she was speaking Lakota. Eventually, you can get beyond this into pure feelings relaying information. On the reservations, I use Native plains sign talk to help bridge language barriers when speaking.

In the Bible, when an apostle taught, people of all races and societies were there and each heard him in their own tongue. This is how it was done: The apostle was very centered as he spoke.

When I stayed with Grandpa Fools Crow, we rarely talked at all. We used sign a lot. Sometimes for several weeks we did not speak directly to each other. He spoke to others who came, and I sat silent. Sometimes I was asked to be a go-between and listen to someone's needs, and tell Grandpa like a translator. Some came who did not need a go-between. They talked in the Indian way through this telepathy.

In our learnings, it might seem that we direct the power. Yet, it is always in participation with the whole. It is in touch with the Spirit in all things. When we use grand powers, it is easy to be awestruck at the vast grandeur. It is almost like keeping your balance on a high cliff edge. Will you fall, or be borne up as on eagle's wings?

In the Christian mystic way you try to live with the Holy Spirit and stay there. Spiritual ability then grows. This is the same as the second Fire Teaching. In some Far Eastern ways you also learn this. Native practice uses nature and has many rituals. Many other ways also have ritual, but all ways recognize that a master no longer needs ritual.

Each Way follows a progression of changes to awareness and perception, elevating consciousness.

One way to look at centering and attainment is that every single thing vibrates at its own *speed.* Every thing is one vast whole, and can be experienced as merely different manifestations of the same thing. Therefore, matter is matter is matter. What differentiates one form of matter from another form are the vibrations, rates, and speed. When we enter a different consciousness, we are altering our own rates, or speed. One way to understand this is to appreciate that the whole Native system is one vast field that vibrates at its own patterns and speeds. To enter that world you must slowly transform your own consciousness over a period of time. The Christian way is its own vast field with particular vibrations and speed giving a different hue to the same knowledge.

When you match up with a field already existing, you are enlightened concerning it. This brings a particular world-view.

When we arrive at the center of creation, I believe that we are matching the vibrations of that level and perceive what is always there: golden-yellow Light.

I believe that we do not always perceive this Light because of the relativity we create, and the way we define self. This is one view that might help you.

I also believe this is like the kingdom of heaven that Jesus said is all around us if we could but perceive it. So I remind you that the content of experiences sometimes distracts us from understanding the nature of experiences.

I will use a friend as an example of this. He needed guidance so we went into the bush in Ontario. We canoed in for eight days and made camp by a clear lake. I made ceremony and saw what he would experience. That night, a physical wolf came to our camp. It walked through camp, glancing at us, and went out on a point of land nearby. The wolf stood on the granite point and howled. My friend was "gone" right then. In spirit, he was on the point of land with the wolf. The wolf began to dance around and my friend joined in. Then, the wolf transported them both in spirit to the High Rockies. Beside another lake, they waited as many wolves came. They all danced together and celebrated life. All the wolves left but one, who turned into a beautiful woman. She taught my friend a song of the wolf. Then she sent him back.

In the morning I told him his wolf-medicine name. Then he told me his vision.

From then on, all he needed to do to enter deep mystical centering was to sing his wolf song. My friend wanted to know if I could find out where the woman lived, because he liked her. He wondered if he could get to know her bodily. His ego still ruled him.

Finding the attraction to be the content rather than the nature of the experience, we sometimes feel the need to associate with others who have similar visionary content. So, warrior lodges and medicine societies are formed. Wolf dreamers sing their wolf songs, and the elk herd together at times. The hue of consciousness attracts us to others with similar hue.

It is all one power. It is reflected many ways. But we say the beaver work together to make their lodge, and even the grizzlies gather at times.

Creatures of dissimilar character stay apart, though. I never used to get along very well with bears. My friend the grizzly-dreamer once offered to let me try on his robe. "See how a bear feels," he said.

I centered myself and he tried the robe on me. I knew what a grizzly felt and had no problem after that getting along with them.

It can all be related to speeds of vibrations. I am trying to explain in a way at harmony with technological thinking. Natives just *do it*.

You might say that a medicine man enters a different perception, changes consciousness, and this brings about ceremonial consciousness.

We just say that we make medicine and things happen. We say that we sit in a fasting circle and the Spirits come.

In older times, the old men could have powerful visions and ceremonial happenings. In some sweats, tiny buffalo would run in and circle the stones before disappearing into the earth. I attended some sweats where a power man was present. One was a strong sweat, and when we came out he advised that we look up. Directly above the lodge the stars themselves formed a giant medicine wheel. There were no other stars in that part of the sky. There is normally no such pattern in the stars. Suddenly, the whole wheel dropped down to the level at which low clouds drift by. A great peace settled over everyone, and awe. This man is alive today.

But, someone prophesied that the older ways would one day go, so I try to concentrate on telling you more about the fundaments.

While learning ritual and custom, I got so many things that one medicine bag was not enough. Today, a medicine bag is often a medium-sized suitcase in which you carry your Pipe in its own leather sack, buffalo horn dipper for sweats, fans, rattles, medicine objects of all kinds. In addition you might have a robe or blanket and a hand-drum to carry. You also get things on-site, such as cherry sticks or sage. It got so bad for me that two bags were not enough. Now I keep nothing, not even a Pipe.

We have the same attitude toward visionary content. We gather it and drag it around like the ritual objects. We do not understand the nature of the experiences.

Visionary experiences can be interpreted, but only by certain people.

Most people do not know what power is like at all. When called upon to pray for healing, a medicine person takes all things are taken into account. From the Symptoms, symbolic meanings are understood. There was a case of a very young boy who suddenly grew gravely ill at a powwow in Canada. The boy had terrible pains in the belly, and a high fever. It seemed to happen from one moment to the next. Conventional non-native medicines were given to him with no effect. The elders were asked, but could not help him. A medicine man was called for, and he couldn't find what it was. Through all this, there was a man sitting, waiting.

He was a Holy Man, but couldn't do anything until asked.

Finally, the parents were ready to take the child to hospital. It seemed nothing could help him. The father asked the Holy Man if he knew anything. The Holy Man smiled and began to pray. In another room of the house, the crying boy suddenly opened his eyes wide, and said clearly, "I am okay now, he asked the Spirits to help me." Within minutes, the fever and pains were gone.

The pains in the belly were bad medicine to destroy the boy's body center and willpower; the fever was to take his mind. Someone hated his father and decided to take it out on the young son.

Surprisingly, the ones who use bad medicine often must make elaborate ritual. The Holy Man comes along and sets things right in moments.

The ones with real Power even used to play games with it to amuse the people. An old man would mark a stick, and throw it into some sage brush. Then he would invite any man who thought he knew something to go get the stick.

Someone would come forward and try to find the stick. The first man would use power to move the stick and perhaps even put a rattlesnake under the sage brush. The second man would be startled, and everyone would laugh. But sometimes, the second man would be a Holy Man. After the stick was moved, he would move the stick back, get rid of the snake, and produce the stick from the sage brush after all. Then everyone chuckled at the first man.

Everything comes back to the balance of the Fire Teachings. Centering.

If you are on a definite path, some people get jealous and even try to hinder or harm you. One defense is deep centering, and renewal in the Spirit in all things.

A clear surface offers no resistance. If ego is in its place, or if you have virtually no ego at all, it cannot be offended and make you react emotionally. There are ways to clear impurities out of yourself. Sometimes the spirits (angelic beings) are invited to do the healing. There are ways to keep bad medicines from affecting you in the physical. There are ways to ensure that your medicines work in the physical. Usually the people who bother others are not so knowledgeable after all. It is like someone learning some martial arts techniques and then challenging Bruce Lee. Bruce Lee fought from inner realization. Such men will always be victorious over those who learn a few technical things.

Most people do not know what true power is. Their minds have not been opened to comprehend. Some people think that power is to have a dream. That is moonlight power. Sunlight obscures moonlight. You often cannot even tell the moon is out when the sun shines. That is the difference of powers.

Power is like when an old man sings a song, and every time that he sings it, half the sky fills with thunderclouds that sit against the wind for hours, making lightning.

Power is like at powwow when mosquitoes are plaguing the people. An old man prays, and asks the mosquitoes to stay across the creek for four days. You can see hordes of mosquitoes swarming across the creek, hungry for blood.

But not one crosses the creek for four days.

When these old men pray, they always start the same way, they say:

Grandfather, pity us, for I am only a weak man! We are pitiful here on earth, pity us.

Their knowledge has made them humble.

Some people want power for its own sake. Some people want fame for its own sake. Some people want to dominate and hurt others. I said earlier that sometimes bad medicine happens. I am going to talk about that now. It might be upsetting.

Uncle Mark told me that one day, about ten years in the future, a man would try to kill me. He would eventually be helped by another old man. I asked Uncle Mark if healing ceremony would be enough to combat their bad medicine. He said for these two men it would not be enough, and that I should use a spiritual weapon of defense. It would not be something I could remove from myself, but something all around me, acting on me. The attack would be a very determined effort by those wishing to charge money and to make non-natives their dogs.

Uncle Mark explained traditional weapons to me, and said that while he was restricted to using things found only on the Turtle Island of North America, my dual heritage would allow me to use things from anywhere in the world.

Then he reviewed with me the knowledge my attacker would have ten years in the future, and the knowledge of the second old man who would be called upon to help. I examined the possibilities, and when I made my choices, I made my defensive weapon in the spirit realm. I left it there, to be used from that realm. Uncle Mark showed me how to carry it with me at all times, but so no one would know I even had it.

I did not even think of it again for ten years.

I was camped on the prairie with my wife, four miles from pavement down a sticky, slurpy, clay road, across a creek, far from anyone. On a clear, sunny day, there was suddenly a violent wind storm just at our camp. It was calm and clear everywhere else, but our camp was being wrecked. I had a dome-shaped mountain tent designed for high winds at high altitudes, but the dome-shaped tent collapsed in these great winds. It was like a small hurricane just where we were. The roof was being torn off a nearby deserted frame house, and my truck was rocking so badly it was in danger of being rolled across the prairie. We dragged ourselves behind a log calf-shed, and I focused to see what was happening. I saw a house as though I was looking in through the roof. I saw an older man with a helper, making medicine in the spirit realm. The helper looked up at me, and told the older man, "He sees us." The older man said clearly, "Doesn't matter, one minute they are dead, anyway."

I took out the weapon and used it on the older man. The man collapsed out of the spirit realm, and his helper fled after him. The winds stopped immediately.

The man did not die. He had a heart attack, and was filled with a melancholy and lassitude that kept him from doing anything in the spirit realm. Eventually, if he reformed his behavior, he would be alright.

He asked another man to go into the spirit realm and remove the weapon so he could be healthy and come after me again. That man saw that this was a just punishment but decided to interfere anyway. The man tried, and he also got hit. This weapon was meant to stay right there until the man reformed. That man sought healing, and would have nothing more to do with it.

A second old man was called. He heard what happened, and sent a helper into the spirit realm to remove the weapon. He thought that if he lost a helper, he could always get more.

The second old man's helper was hit, and so was the second old man. Because of foresight, I had built all this into the weapon. Anyone even associated with trying to remove it would also get hit. The second old man was bedridden.

The second old man tried to get people together to harm me. Finally, after several weeks of just clearing out bad medicine daily, I got really fed up. I drove right to the second old man's house, and walked in. He was in bed in the living room, all alone. He remarked, "It's funny you show up at the only time I am alone for an hour."

Of course, I would not show up when he was surrounded by helpers. I thought it should speak volumes that I even could show up when he was alone, but he tried to use power from his sickbed. I merely stopped him and left. The next day he decided to leave the reservation to rest elsewhere.

I do not feel too bad about saying we sometimes must defend ourselves. If a dog tries to bite you, it is a natural reaction to kick it so it stops.

These things might sound fantastic to some, and are not exactly everyday things. But they do sometimes happen. When I stayed with Fools Crow he watched over the house and people. One day we were driving to Gordon, Nebraska, for shopping. I suddenly jumped while driving, having had a sudden seeing. Grandpa asked in great concern, "What did you see?"

I motioned in sign to wait and he patiently waited. I had seen someone trying to do something to my Pipe in the spirit realm. I moved its essence, and sealed it up. The Pipe, I left where it was. I told Grandpa a man was trying to steal my Pipe, and he understood what I meant (someone tried to interfere with my spiritual ability). He frowned deeply, angry that anyone would dare try anything at his place. Eventually, I let the attackers come to my Pipe in the spirit realm, because I had safely removed the essence. This way, I saw who they all were. I could always make another physical Pipe; the essence is what matters. I am the Pipe.

Sometimes I have been led somewhere to watch over someone. I was called to the Teaching Mountain once. It is where people have Vision Quest. I took along a woman that I was helping to prepare for a quest, as this promised to be educational. She was my wife.

At the mountain, we found a middle-aged Native man from a different reservation. He had a young white woman with him. Weird things kept happening to her. Now, she was ill and the doctors could not find a cause. The man said he was going to sweat with her, and doctor her. I suspected the man right away, because you always take along a chaperone so a decent woman is not compromised. The man had a whole reservation to choose from, no matter the urgency. So he was either the one who made her ill, or he did not respect her because of her race. In either case, he was not fit to treat her. He did not respect her at all.

He invited us to attend the sweat, and I replied that I would attend, but not my wife. I explained to her what was happening, and that it could even get a little dangerous. When the man lit the fire to heat the stones, I prayed that the Spirits would see the right thing done. An owl began to hoot to me from partway up the mountain. I invited it to join us, and it flew down to the lodge. It landed in a dead tree not ten feet from the roaring fire. It stared at the lodge, and the man, and back up the mountain. It hooted and talked all afternoon, and deep into the night. In all, it stayed at least eight hours, hooting all the time. It stopped only during the sweat, but resumed immediately afterwards. Once during the sweat, it hooted to me.

Since the owl was already there, I said I would like to bring into the sweat an owl tail fan that I used. The man looked at me for a moment, considering, then agreed. He did not see any particular medicine around me, so was not worried. I smudged the lodge with the fan, and planned to hold it through the whole ceremony. But the man looked nauseated and insisted that I remove the fan. So I set it outside.

I asked the Spirits to show me what was wrong with the woman. I saw a vision of something put into her heart in the spirit realm. It was very awful just to see, and I pitied her having those sickly things acting upon her. In my turn, I prayed out loud that the bad medicine would be safely removed. In my innermost recesses of being, I prayed that the bad medicine would be shot right back into whoever had put it there.

When the sweat ended, the man said he knew I had a seeing. He admitted that it surprised him. Now, he was going to take her alone into his tent, and I was not welcome. I let it go, because the owl was there, and I was sure what would happen anyway. He would not begin his medicine until the owl left, so I asked the owl to check one last time if all was well, and then it left.

In the morning, he said the woman was cured but that now the damned thing was in him. He left soon after to seek healing for himself.

What a bastard. He made her ill so she would be grateful to him for healing her. But, she was free once more.

My friend the grizzly-dreamer told me how he was once shot with sleeping medicine at a Sundance, where we are all supposed to be brothers. He started to get drowsy, and his mind grew unclean. He staggered into a tipi, and collapsed. He knew certain people were laughing at him. They wanted to take him out of the ceremony because they were jealous.

They stopped smiling when he came out a minute later, clear, strong, and in his medicine power Then they stayed out of his way.

In the spirit realm, something gets done to you and this sleeping medicine is the effect in body. It can wear off in several days, but for that time you are too unaware to even seek help.

Around the Holy Ones, who have real power, you do not even speak harshly, and never keep pushing until they lose their temper. One day two women began to fight physically in Fools Crow's house. I grabbed one to restrain her. Grandpa leaped out of his armchair, ran across the room, grabbed the other by the hair, and threw her bodily out of the house. She had started the troubles. Not bad for a ninety-four-year-old man.

Everyone in the house seemed to hold their breath for four days to see what would happen. The woman who had been thrown out had a new four-wheel-drive truck she was proud of. She did not have insurance. Although it was June, the police report later said she must have hit some black ice. As she drove along a straight, level road, her truck began to flip and roll over. It was a total wreck but she stood up without a scratch on her. Black ice also can mean a medicine power. The Native police have a sense of humor.

There are good, warm-hearted people around. But there are also some two-faced people who smile as they try to make you their dog. They try to make you have dreams, and seeings. They try to use you like the second old man who sent in a helper to remove my defensive weapon. If they lose a dog, they do not care. There are more. That is how some treat their helpers.

Sometimes strangers have walked up to me and offered me objects. They say the Spirits want me to have it, and it is so special I should not tell anyone. That is so no one can tell you differently. This is one way they try to get something into your house to begin to work their medicine on you. It is best to be careful what gifts you accept, or keep. Even the mystic eagle feather that I asked for as a sign was to be released when I learned the meaning. Today, I have no objects at all.

Well, about this making of dogs. I am telling you because it does sometimes go on. I am not saying it is everyone, or even most. I am not saying it is in every nation. But all you need to do is run into one of these people and you can have problems. The blind loyalty of these dogs is like the physical animal. A dog does not care if its master is good or evil. If the master says kill, the dog tries to do it. No questions asked.

The teaching tales tell us of this. The story might say there was once an evil bear, who kept the buffalo from the people so that they were starving to death. This means that an evil bear-medicine man kept the good-medicine nourishment of sharing and co-operation from the people and they were dying spiritually.

In the tales, a young boy who is a mystic hero usually comes, kills the bear, sets the buffalo free, and feeds the people.

The tales are about creatures, but imply people. They are about life's lessons and spiritual integrity. Nowadays, things have changed. In older times, liars were killed. If a man took a woman alone to a sweatlodge and seduced or even raped her, they were both killed. He was killed because of his act. She was killed because she jeopardized the reputation of good women by acting as though this was acceptable behavior. She placed herself in that position of vulnerability against traditional ways.

If someone went a little wrong, they were given chances to reform. Even the men who tried to kill me are alive today. They have a chance to reform. The council could decide if someone should be killed because they will never reform. Banishment was another fate.

In older times, every part of your traditional costume was something of sacred importance to you. No one would imagine just getting an owl fan and dancing with it. No man started braiding his hair unless he was qualified for this. Hair grows like knowledge, and we gather together the strands of experiences and braid them together into something stronger than any strand could be. That is what braids mean.

A lot of traditional culture has been lost, but many are trying to get it back again. But even Wovoka the Paiute prophet predicted that native Peoples would get on a new earth where there were no non-natives, except a few. I believe this is still coming. The symbols are interpreted that way. The new earth is a new consciousness, or reality.

All this bad medicine arises from fear. In spiritual development, ego-fires must be dealt with. Ego can create fear. It is fear that we might only be just one more part of the whole, and not so special after all. It is fear that if we surrender to spiritual guidance, we might somehow lose our self. In terms of the teachings, it is the man who shoves others aside to take what he thinks is a favored position at the Fire. He seeks to demonstrate his self-importance, just as a bad medicine man tries to be the top man. He does not know that the real top man is he who truly considers himself just another part of the whole, and no more important than any other part.

In terms of sociological influence, the ones wanting power are those who want to be the center of attention, not the center of the circle of harmony. It is the man who throws too much wood on the fire because he is really afraid of the dark. This means that he acts aggressively and in an ego-centered manner because he fears facing his own self in relation to the vast universe. He fears to see that his life is only very small and brief, after all. He seeks attention in whichever ways he can get it. This is imbalance.

When everyone is sitting in a circle around a campfire, and sharing equally in the warmth of the fire and the warmth of togetherness, the self-proclaimed "warrior" strides up and disrupts the whole circle by his behavior. He is not a true warrior after all. He is just an ego-centered, self-absorbed person. A true warrior knows his heart.

Likewise, to enter the Spirit in all things, we must be willing to participate. This is a fundamental law of consciousness. Sometimes, people fear to lose their uniqueness. I had the same fear and asked for an impossible sign, the eagle feather. Some people throw more wood on their inner fires and act more demandingly and with more cravings.

Individuality will not be lost when we walk our path in a sacred manner. Our illusions will be lost as they are purified from us. We still exist as the same person. It is a liberation not to be chained to mortal limitations anymore. It is like in the Bible: We must overcome the world, overcome our mortal nature.

We can still use the body realm, and enjoy the sensations. But we are not confined to that level.

Many of our actions and reactions are based upon over-emphasis of the ego. If your ego is in its place, you will not act as before. If insulted, you do not need to react immediately with aggressive behavior because ego is offended. You are in a more dispassionate center. It is not emotionally governed.

From this smooth surface of cleared consciousness, you can react immediately by going deeper into centering to use spiritual ability. You can choose decisively to react with anger or emotion. It is not automatic, but a conscious choice.

Keeping your center amidst turmoil is one aspect of mystical attainment. You can still react with violence if essential, but it is a conscious choice. It is not a reaction to external conditions based upon fear or emotional response. The situation is weighed against a greater movement of the whole. All the implications are known. When a true warrior chooses to fight, it is with everything that he has, and knows. Likewise, the true warrior can walk through the midst of his enemies and they cannot stop him.

Jesus also did this. When outraged people came to kill him, He simply walked through them and no one could try to stop him. Yet when it was His time, He let Himself be killed. People do not like to think of Jesus as a warrior. But I think of Him that way. He was a warrior whose fight was for spiritual truth in the world. If He had just materialized as did the bringer of the Pipe, we would be more intimidated by that. But He was born of flesh, and rose in light and consciousness, to show us that we could do this also.

The true warrior acts, and then retreats back into himself again.

When I visited Fools Crow before living with him, there was a young white man also visiting. He came to where several of us were sitting in a tipi, talking. He said that he wanted to walk along the dry stream bed and gather fallen branches. He wanted to drag them back to the house, and then cut them up for the old folks to use in the woodstove in winter. He asked me what I thought of that, if it was a good idea.

We all sat quiet a moment, then I told him, "When the old man puts the wood in the stove in the dead of winter, he will recall you. Do it because you want to do it, and then forget about it."

He wanted to be invited to sit in a special place of honor for doing this. He wanted to be thanked profusely. He sat, thinking, for a long while. But he never cut any wood.

Uncle Mark, my favorite teacher, spent many years trying to get teachings into my thick head. He taught me to peel red willow to expose the inner bark for the Pipe mixture. He was the only person on earth with whom I shared the secrets of my own Pipe mixture. When it was all done, I never thanked him. Neither would he have expected it. He told me that he taught me because that was part of his vision. I learned because it was part of mine. As people, our personal lives did not matter compared with the desire to fulfill sacred design.

The true warrior can perform his acts and then retreat into himself because ego is in its balanced place. He needs only perform his actions because it is his choice. He does not wait for the people to encourage him or to praise him. If encouragement or praise comes, fine. It is not why he acts.

The true warrior examines his choices deliberately. He centers himself and silently wonders. If the problem is sociological, he acts knowing the greater spiritual implications. This is like the Oriental way of following the *Tao,* seeing if your acts are within the Way.

Is my act going to strengthen harmony within the whole, or cause discord? Ego has no place in such a deliberation. While we are yet growing, we might fight the enemy to gain rank and recognition. That is the body level we are at then, and we must yet mature into a real warrior. We act from the level that we have reached.

On the Red Road, the east and west can be said to symbolize external or objective things, and internal or subjective things. East and west are external physical reality and internal subjective spirituality. Through outer, physical experiences we acquire spiritual growth. From spiritual growth, we acquire new types of experiences in the physical. Each acts upon the other until the mid-point of balance is reached: centering. Then, there is no gap between manifest and Spirit. Then, we may be constantly spiritually aware to some degree.

Where a lot of people fail on Vision Quest, or even in sweatlodge, is that they are doing it for external physical reasons. They want to belong, or ego just wants it. They want acceptance from the group, or praise.

Staying in a fasting circle for days without food and water is the external part. The reason for doing so is the internal spiritual part. If you are fasting for reasons of ego, which belongs to body realm, you will not succeed.

Some people fast for the right reasons and have miraculous things happen. My wife, whom I helped to prepare, had thunder and lightning follow her all the way up the mountain. When she made her circle, it rained only there. I stood two feet outside the circle and stayed dry. She was soaking wet in a downpour. We say the Thunderbeings blessed her fasting circle. Everyone else there had trouble with wood ticks, but she never saw one. Others shivered in the cold night. When she was done, she half-complained that she thought she was meant to be suffering. Yet she was warm and secure. She found it an easy fasting, though it was two days and nights with no food or water.

Yet, I did not follow traditional ways with her. The sweatlodges at the Teaching Mountain were all used and no one would share them because she was white. The other people had very bad hearts that day. We had sweated on the rez the night before, so I simply had her pick some sage. After she wiped herself down with sage, I just prayed with the Pipes and took her up the mountain. That evening, we saw dozens and dozens of Spirits going to where she fasted. One other man fasting on the same part of the mountain said he saw a very old Holy Man sitting on the rocks above her, watching over her the whole time.

She had prepared for a year for her two-day fast. When I brought her down, we simply smoked both Pipes. I had prepared berry sauce for her from cherries, and she ate slowly. Several of the men who wouldn't share the lodges came over and shook her hand, and wanted to meet the white woman who did things the old way, properly. They regretted their earlier bigotry.

If you are prepared, you do not even need a Pipe. You do not even need to mark a fasting circle. You just pray, and things happen. Some people have many helpers carry all their sacred things up the mountain, but they do not have such strong experiences. Some merely fast so they qualify to Sundance. Because they fasted for the wrong reason, they usually have a hard time, or even collapse, at Sundance.

If you have done anything of worth, others will say it about you. If you have done good work, they might say to each other in times of need, "Go to him, he doesn't charge money like some, he respects women, and talks straight all the time.

All this is in the Bible as well. Jehovah said to Moses, "If you make an altar, make it of mellowed earth. If you make a stone altar, do not cut, shape, or change the stone in any way as that is a desecration to Me."

This means, if you make your body a temple through the harmony of mellowed earth ways, this is pleasing to Jehovah. This is the humble way of living in harmony, without ego. This is a Fire Teaching.

If you worship with Stone, mystic spirituality, do not impose man's will (ego-desires) upon the natural perceptions and consciousness. It means, whether you follow the Red Road of living the balance of harmony until spiritual awareness comes, or follow the mystic path of seeking the higher Light, live in natural harmony and light. Do not try to change the Stone by imposing ego-desires upon spiritual expressions.

This is why Holy Ones will always triumph over evil ones. The fact that a man gets a little power and is corrupt, means that he cannot reach the fullest potential of spiritual awareness because of his imbalances. The Holy Man who has set aside ego can go further into the mystical center.

The Christians also say that one Holy Man sits praying, and a thousand demons cannot distract him.

Of course, we are not born holy, but grow more holy. Sometimes we encounter problems along the way. To me, power is a side issue. Your inner state is the thing of interest. Whether you follow the Red Road or the Black Road, you will realize that spiritual ability comes through harmony and being able to generate Light. It is clear consciousness in participation with the whole.

SEVEN

STONE IS PERCEPTION, A HUE OF CONSCIOUSNESS.
DIFFERENT STONES REPRESENT DIFFERENT HUES OF
CONSCIOUSNESS, OR MEDICINE-DREAMS.

You may hear about circles of stones all around North America. There are thousands, if you count tipi rings. In older times, stones were sometimes used to hold down the edges of the tipi. Some stone circles are altars, the so-called medicine wheels.

There is a lot of interest now in different kinds of stone and crystals. This reflects people's interest and yearning to understand consciousness and perception. One sees more art and craft works with stones and crystals on them. In older times this was not done. It is a new thing.

Many stone altars are not wheels at all. One is a giant turtle, and another is a large circle with a spiral path in it.

Before you can put stones together into a fasting circle, you should have taken actual journeys and encountered fundamental consciousness. This does not mean sleep-dreams.

Before you even help to make stone altars, you must be a master of at least one Way. Before that, you are not attained enough and would only be assembling your illusions in a place where they can harm others. That energy needs to be purified out.

Some people are putting together their body center as they approach the balance of the Fire Teachings, and mistakenly think they are putting together their inner medicine wheel. This is not so. They have encountered the outer circle of the altar; but since it is all that mind can encompass from mortal limitations, they mistakenly believe that are putting together the wheel.

Stone is perception, a hue of consciousness. The medicine altars have different shapes for a reason. They each have different reasons for being. Each stone can be said to reflect and represent a reflection of the one power. The consciousness, or medicine, is associated with the stone, but is not in it. We say that if you enter the altars in the right way, you will perceive things. When you enter the state between manifest and ethereal realms, you perceive things. You can understand how the parts relate, because you have experienced the whole.

Before going to the center, I wondered about symbols. Gradually, I understood more. I went to a medicine altar in Saskatchewan. It had just been returned to Native possession and the keepers wondered how I knew about it. I said I needed to pray there, and they guided me to it. It is a very large circle with a central cairn and five spokes. It is more than twice as large as the famous medicine wheel in Wyoming.

I made ceremony and entered the wheel. I realized right away that something was wrong. I looked around and found out that while it was in non-native possession the central cairn had been dug up and the sacred offerings removed. They sat in museums in drawers somewhere. I simply left, for it is no longer a whole thing and is a distortion of its original purpose.

This happens often. Now that the non-native world is also getting interested in the mystic, it is too late for many of the sacred ways. They are already gone. Hardly any stone altar is left undisturbed.

When my wife fasted in a circle of stones, she collected them from special places and we carried them up the mountain. That is fine; she is qualified for that because she reached fundamental perception. But if you can clear your mind and enter true balance, your circle is one of pure perception and consciousness. That is the real old way.

The world is your fasting circle, marked by the horizon and the directions along that horizon. You are the center of this great circle of mystery and life. Grandeur surrounds you.

You might decide with intellect that you want to fast four days and nights. So what happens if you get an answer to your question right away? This happened to me once. I had made my circle and began to pray when I was told something, and advised to go back down (from the physical height of the mountain and the heights of consciousness).

I stayed because I wanted to fulfill my vow. A small butterfly darted before me. When it knew it had my attention it flew around behind me. A terrific blow struck my back, shoving me forward several feet. I spun around, and there was only the tiny butterfly, hovering. It struck me again and I gathered my things and left. I later found out there was somewhere I should be the next morning and that I could not have been there if I stayed fasting.

I can't stress enough that if you follow customs and ritual only in the outer form of having things, you will not get very far. If you have the inner traditional awareness, or mystical centering, you do not need things. It is true that the path of ritual is rather secure. But the attractiveness of having a sense of belonging, and using sacred things, can be detrimental to higher transcendences. We encounter ritual and ritualistic objects; but once we have established ourselves in that consciousness, we should be able to go beyond needing these things.

Can you imagine being in need, but feeling helpless because you do not have your rattle with you? Ritual can help open us up. All these magical objects open the door for us. Or do they?

When I stayed with Grandpa Fools Crow, he used ritual or not, depending upon the circumstances.

Uncle Mark said if you have to sweat, or pray, or even Vision Quest, and you do not have a Pipe, never mind. As long as your heart is good the Spirits hear you.

What you should understand is this: Development, following a path, is to grow in awareness through perception and elevated consciousness. This generates Light. Native ways are a system. They were given to a group of peoples. They are sacred ways, but only one system of sacred ways. There are other systems, religions. Each way focuses on a slightly different aspect of the total knowledge. Some ways contain more of the wholeness of life, and they encompass more knowledge than some other ways.

When a person becomes knowledgeable, he or she is faced with the problem of translating that inner knowledge into a coherent form that less knowledgeable people can grasp. Usually, cultural context is used and deepens symbolism. Not having had the experiences, you do not really know. So, the sage or mystic describes how he came to transcend. He describes how it felt, what he saw, and how his concept of self and world changed. This creates a *picture* of attainment.

Attainment is really a process. It is a change of perception as consciousness is elevated, or speeded up.

When we recognize that the horizon marks a boundary, and that we are standing at the center of all points on the horizon, this fits perfectly with other understandings and so we create symbols. Each part of our experiences could be put into symbols. Ultimately, we could end up with a system so bogged down by symbols that few could grasp them all to form a coherent understanding of attainment and the whole.

By studying the symbols, and how they interrelate, some try to transcend for themselves. This is a system, a way, a path, a walk through life's mysteries.

There is no Way, there is no Path, there is no Tao, there is no Red Road, there is no Black Road.

These are words to describe something inside us, reflecting to and from the world around us. The truth is indescribable. Nothing more can be said about it than that. Yet, we manage to find thousands of words for something we all know deep inside us if we could but uncover the inner self. I will have to use symbols again. See what a problem it is?

We say that there are Four Directions. These are said to correspond to four parts of self. The west is spirit, north is mind, east is body, south is heart.

We say that we must balance these parts of our self. This is a process. It is a perception that we learn. We say that we have a manifest realm and a body life in that realm. We say that we have a dream realm and a mental realm. We have the centering and loving warmth of participating fully with nature.

If we have these different aspects of self, we can logically understand that spirit is not created at the moment that we first perceive it from body states. Our own spirit must already exist on its own realm. In fact, it is the "familiar still, small voice" we speak of, guiding us to embrace our own spiritual self, our own spirit, leading the body level to realizations. For everyone does have their very own

Guardian Angel watching over them. It is our very own spiritual self gently guiding us to realize its presence.

To feel the full sensations of body levels is one perception. To perceive that we can act with volition in lucid dreams is one perception. To know that we can use powers from the manifest when we enter spiritual awareness is one perception. To know that there is a core of awareness underlying all these is one perception.

These are the first four stones we place in the sweatlodge pit, for the Four Directions, the four parts of sell, the simplest medicine wheel.

We call it growth to change perceptions and elevate consciousness. "Now then," you can ask, "Is it that the trick of all this is to change perceptions?" Yes, that is pretty much the trick.

In symbolic terms, it is to move from one stone to the next in your medicine wheel as you learn. Eventually you learn different perceptions and arrive at the center. In the end, you look back and know it was all stone, no matter where you stood within the wheel. It takes most of a lifetime to truly understand.

These Stones are all perceptions, different hues of consciousness. And so, having all these "parts" to a whole being, we cannot let the manifest level dominate the total being. We should also try to become more spiritually aware while enjoying our brief time of body life.

How someone changes perceptions begins with feelings. When I conduct ceremony I begin by changing my mood and feelings. I feel a positive certainty without being certain of any one thing. It is a very calm thing.

Music also changes our mood and feelings. So we should be careful what music we listen to. If you sing the sacred songs of the Four Winds, it evokes a certain mood through tone and word. It changes feelings to a prescribed perception. If you sing a sacred Pipe song, it changes feelings to a different prescribed perception. Each time, feelings help us to change perceptions and elevate consciousness.

In all ceremonies, perception changes and indicates that consciousness has changed. The how and the why of the changes are what we call the different medicines.

All the rituals and objects were designed to aid us in learning to change perceptions and consciousness. So the Red Road is not a concrete thing. As a product, or an end in itself, it is not real. Some people treat it as a thing, with concrete substance like an interstate highway. It is a set of words to describe our changes in perception and consciousness. Thus, the Red Road, and all Ways, are not real things in themselves but hues of the same consciousness permeating all of creation.

If you ask good medicine people, they will tell you that Native ways are but one system among many. Many cultures do not understand their own ways, so they begin to turn to Native ways. It has been said that Native peoples should teach the world. This is so. But no one said to convert the world to Native ways.

It was said, be honest about Native ways, and people will understand more of the truth of life, including their own ways previously not understood.

It should not even be debated which ways hold which amounts of truth. There is an underlying grain of truth in all religions. Which exact grain various long-ago mystics focused their teachings on gives rise to the differences in religions today. We cannot discern the distinctions from the darkness of mortal mind.

Symbols are like the paint that we use to cover something. If I want to tell you about my car, I say the paint is blue. Now you picture a blue car. Ah, but it is a *light* blue car. Now you picture that. But it is a light blue car with a white roof. Now you imagine that.

I want to tell you about centering. So, I use the directions, and the four parts of self. I talk about teachings, and wholeness.

I still own a blue car with a white roof, but the description gets more and more detailed. Eventually, you can know an awful lot about my car. But to really know it, you must see it and drive it yourself. Centering is that way. You can read about it, hear about it, but you have to do it to really know. Some things about driving my car cannot be put into words.

You can come to form a mood about transcendence. Once you formulate a mood, your inner feelings are drawn in the right way and perception begins to change. Maybe you even transcend.

So what are symbols but descriptive words and objects to help us change levels of consciousness and perception?

So we have this manifest world. Every last thing, action, phenomenon can be seen as symbolic. What a flood of information! This is the flood of Noah.

Noah took with him male and female of each creature and sailed over the turbulent waters. I believe the flood happened physically. It is symbolic at the same time. Ceremony is like that: literally true and symbolically true as well. (Symbolically could also be expressed as "conveying significance.") Deeply mystical events are like that.

Noah made wine, took off all his clothing and sat drunk in his tent, unaware of the world. This means that he acquired the ability to go beyond body limitations, for this is what wine represents. He removed the clothing that represents customs and tradition of his people before the flood. He was naked, without custom or tradition. He sat in the tent of his sheltering reality, and went beyond.

The ability to transcend body limitations is the symbolic wine of Christianity. So, Jesus turned water of wholeness and one-ness into the wine of the ability to go beyond, by placing it into Stone pots of fundamental perception. He later said that the wine was His very blood, the stuff of life to Him.

And to the person who overcomes the world is given a white stone, and a white robe, and their name is written in Light forever in heaven.

When we begin to understand, we form a coherent picture of the whole and transcend. Mellowed earth, prepare for the seed of Light. Jesus talked about the seeds falling on hard and mellowed earth. All of these symbols can lead us somewhere.

In the end, we will find that there is only one direction: the one in which we face.

We will find that there is no above and below except as separated by perception. We will find there are no parts of self, but one whole self merely separated into different levels of perception.

I was talking about symbols. Before Marie died, she told me when her death would be. She pointed out particular people to me. She said that they were old-time good-heart people. She also said that when the last of these people died, please leave the rez, as it would get very bad for a while.

It used to be universally known that when camping, Native people made a very small fire. We sat very close to it. Non-natives made a very large fire and sat far back from it. First of all, this means that Native people were much more in tune with the natural world and feared it very little, if at all. They did not need to push back a dark and fearsome night, because they were warmed by inner participation with the Spirit in all things. Non-natives, out of touch with the natural world and Spirit, threw more wood on the fire.

In emotions, Native people of strong heart build a small fire, but sit very close to it. We stay in touch with warm-heart feelings. Old-time Native peoples were not emotional, but very passionate through heart. Non-natives often build a very large fire of emotions and ego-demands, and sit far away from heart-feelings. Today, young people of all races seem to build the largest fires of all.

Today, fewer people understand living by a small fire. It is the second Fire Teaching. It brings the purification represented by the driving snows in my youthful experience. This relates directly to understanding your place in the cosmos. If you build a large fire to push back the fearsome darkness, you are really trying to push back the fear of facing the ultimate solitude of your mortal condition. You feel alone, vulnerable, and perhaps small in the overall pattern of life.

If you are centered and at peace in the universe, you need only a tiny fire and you sit close to it. You need be less emotional in life, but your passions run deep, strong, and clear. They are heart-felt truths about your direct relation to the universe and your place in it. You are at home everywhere—alone perhaps, but never lonely. Even in death, the final change that we recognize from mortal limit, you are at peace because you are going home, to the spiritual center.

In older times, fire was not a roaring thing. But no one froze to death. That was all we needed, then.

There are times to build a large fire. The fire to heat the stones for sweatlodge must be large. This means that we need our intensity to be able to transcend. But we recall our heart always. The true warrior that I talk about lives by heart, knows his heart, and will die by heart. If you live and die by your heart, you are living and dying by your personal truth of existence. How can you not be at peace then? These are some more truths about Fire.

As far as knowledge goes, it is something sacred to know about Fire. Fire touches all of our lives. We respect not only those who make their fires in the right way, but we also respect those who can make a much hotter fire from the same materials we would use. Their fire always seems to get the stones hotter, faster. This is knowledge of Fire.

Unfortunately, there are a lot of so-called medicine men who cannot even start a fire. They pour gasoline, kerosene, or used motor oil on the wood. Then they stand back and toss lit matches at it. They try to have you believe that they have knowledge.

Likewise, they accept gifts, and even get their helpers to suggest money and gift-giving to you. Most religious ways through the ages have had their pretenders. Somehow, you will feel which are the real ones. Listen to your heart, judge them by heart.

This is what Uncle Mark meant when he said you can have ceremony even without the sacred Pipe. Live by heart. If you live by heart, the warmth eases the darkness of human solitude. You might well ask, "If development, growth, is a matter of changing perceptions and consciousness, then what makes living by heart better than any other perception?" Good question.

Living by heart generates warmth and thus Light, and eases us into embracing more of the whole. Ego closes consciousness and shrinks the field of perception. Upon dying, we each will change consciousness. We can expand consciousness and embrace more of the whole. So, it is spiritual survival to live by heart. We will go to a better place.

When we die, and consciousness opens, we can weigh ourselves, our own life acts, against the standard of the whole. If we have lived some degree of truth and have a strong, good heart, the transition is smoother. We freely embrace Light and Spirit. When we are confronted with the truth of one-ness of all things, the Holy Spirit, we realize the improper manner we may have lived in. At this time, past errors can come to our awareness, and we see them clearly. It is not that our entire life flashes before our eyes, but the grave errors against the Light become clear to us.

Jesus called these sins against the Holy Spirit. When faced with such acts, we do indeed feel a burning much like moments of embarrassed humiliation we can feel in body, but it is much more intense and agonizing. This is the cleansing Fire that can burn within us. During body life, the mystic goes through this. He or she gets cleansed or purified along the way. Others encounter it only in death.

Because we touch the Spirit in all things, however briefly in death, we can try to make this a more fluid thing by living more spiritually. We will become lucid and aware in death, as we are balanced between the fading manifest world and the suddenly illuminated ethereal realm of spiritual being.

The center is the mid-point between mortal human awareness and spiritual being. If we live more balanced and centered, we are more in touch with the spiritual realm. Yet, we can fully enjoy our physical nature. The mystic carries this learning so far that some drop body and travel through this mid-point between realms as a sphere of Light. It is pure awareness that we perceive as Light.

Light is awareness. The road to generating Light is through the Fire Teachings.

When I was very young, I constantly demanded of Uncle Mark why could I not come "home" to the reservation to live. Why was I living in the dominant society? He always said, "One day I'll explain, when you are older." One day he replied, "If I tell people, they won't understand me. You will find the right words to use."

If you asked Uncle Mark what was the truth of existence, the right way to live, what power is, what the Spirits do, almost any question, he would have said, "Live by heart." From that statement, you are supposed to be able to figure all this out yourself. You ponder, strive, and quest, until you know. This is traditional attitude.

If you asked Grandpa Fools Crow about medicines, life, Spirit, visions, the Pipe, anything at all he most likely would have told you to go Sundance.

What he would have meant, is that if you spend several years learning Native philosophy and language, begin to go to sweatlodge and learn its truths for several years, or decades, and eventually Vision Quest several times over the course of years, you might one day Sundance to pierce the realms. After piercing the different levels, you might understand these things one day.

People hear the words and in two months they go several times to sweats, fast one night, and the following week Sundance. They will have learned little in that time.

When you sweat, you are told to pray hard. All the implications of fire, emotion, spiritual centering, are supposed to be gradually understood through this. The traditional mind understands the implications. The non-traditional mind hears only the words. Some Native people have non-traditional minds.

Spiritual language is both factual and symbolic at the same time. If I advised that certain objects be thrown into a fast river just before it empties into the ocean, while praying intensely, I meant this literally as the ceremony.

I *also* meant that the healing medicine to remove the bad medicine would be to cross to the other realm of Spirit almost to the watery one-ness while praying, and the bad medicine would be cast into the void, never to return. This is done from body.

Because the symbolic value and literal fact match in ceremony, one can not just make up a ceremony. Using only brain to invent a ceremony will bring only confusions. Brain is only part of the whole being. During ceremony, it is cleared of activity. So how can you think up a ceremony?

Every thing in creation, every action and series of actions, all weather phenomena are seen to have inherent meaning. During ceremony, this meaning is truth.

The man who first took me to sweatlodge advised me, "You can get too caught up in the meanings of everything. Some try to see the meaning of everything, even going to the bathroom. You have to get back out of that and just live your life."

I went to visit a friend who has a nature school. His helpers and advanced students approached me during the visit. They said they feared their teacher was bothered by bad medicine. They said there were some bone artifacts which they believed had the bad medicine in them.

They asked if I would take the bones into the nearby woods and bury them at the foot of the oak tree. I simply refused. As far as I was concerned, the matter was closed. They did not even bring any tobacco for the Spirits. They asked me twice, which is also improper behavior. They asked me what I would do with these things to get rid of them. I said that I would throw them in a fast river just before it emptied into the ocean while praying all the while. They said, "But, our teacher says oak is the strongest tree, and will absorb bad things. We don't understand."

I replied in true traditional fashion and said, "I know you don't understand," and walked away.

If I Wrote from my inner Native self, this whole book would be like that. But I have a non-native side to my being as well. I write to try to explain traditional concepts in a way conducive to the European-American understanding.

€IGHT

*MEDICINES AND RITUAL ARE AN AID. THEY HELP A
PERSON TO CHANGE PERCEPTIONS AND CONSCIOUSNESS.
BUT ONE CAN GO BEYOND THE NEED OF RITUAL.*

True Native religion and spiritual development realizes that we are focusing on the material world and this fixation must be eventually transcended. This is a basic assumption made freely.

We know that to break the barriers of mortal perception, seeing only what is affecting us while in body, we can use ritual to help open us up. It is said that it takes at least thirty years to learn Native religion. Then we begin to understand life and Spirit.

For this reason we do not expect anyone to be spiritually mature until they are in their fifties, sixties, or seventies. A few who start early might begin to understand in their forties, if they have done almost nothing else in life but seek spiritually.

Just because a person is in their fifties or sixties does not mean they have adequately purified themselves. You notice a man in his sixties who has a large following and many helpers. This does not mean he is holy, just popular. He might even be a fame-seeking egotist who wants a lot of recognition and gifts.

It is widely known that one can go beyond need of ritual. It is not talked about a lot, but it is known. If someone has transcended, traveled beyond body realms, divided consciousness, affected cures, that person begins to do things more and more without ritual.

Sometimes you encounter someone who, as a part of the learning process, does some things without ritual or ritualistic ceremony. As he grows older, and becomes stable in spiritual awareness, the abilities he exhibited earlier will come through again. Just because he did some things without ceremony when young, does not mean that he can always do so. When he matures spiritually he likely will do so.

Some young men (under forty), do conduct their own sweats and even put themselves into a fasting circle. They transcend and go off alone to fast. They are guided by Spirit. This is more similar to the way that Jesus taught. He said that His followers should be more like Him. He went alone into wilderness to fast, and climbed mountains alone to pray.

In the Native way, it is more usual to seek the guidance of an elder. It was said, for instance, that if Fools Crow agreed to help you fast, you would have a strong experience. His prayers would ensure that you had a strong experience.

People seem not to realize this about leaving ritual behind. Some people say they will use the Pipe until the day they die. Well, that is not even the point. The Pipe is also something to get beyond. When I asked if I might have a long-stemmed Pipe, Uncle Mark told me to learn it for seven years, and then begin to set it aside. If you can acquire the consciousness intended, you will not always need the Pipe. To be a free man means also to be freed of these things.

A lot of people do not realize that when you go to an old Holy Man for help, he is only making ritualistic ceremony for your benefit. He doesn't need it. It helps you to open up; he is already opened.

When you carry your Pipe into a natural area with the intention of making ceremony, you have already created the mood through your *intent.* Each step helps you to feel that you are drawing nearer to the place where manifest and ethereal meet. You think it is because the Pipe is holy and has awesome powers. It is true that objects can have their natural energies augmented by a Holy Man's prayer. But primarily the opening is within us. We can perceive that the Pipe opens us up. The Pipe, or ritual, is a buffer zone. If we did these things without the Pipe, we would have to face the truth: The ethereal is always there, spiritual consciousness is always within reach. We can feel ceremonial consciousness anytime we choose to do so through changing perceptions and feelings. To keep these realizations from crashing in on us, and disrupting our physical life, we have a buffer zone in consciousness, a limit to mortal awareness.

There is not one thing that I have yet encountered in ritual, song, ceremony, or tradition that I did not first experience under the guidance of my teachers without objects or ritual. There was nothing new for me in Sundance ceremony but a cumbersome enactment of going to the center.

I have never thought that I am an unusual person. I have thought it is an unusual world that needs these things and fears their own spiritual selves.

Anyone learning about Light will leave behind what they once knew. You will discover new things. Jesus also said to be in the world, but not of the world. I used to feel sorry for some of the old men of power. I knew they had to live in certain ways and I wondered if they ever missed doing some of the things other men did. But it was their choice, accepted in youth as a lifelong commitment. Being a mystic is for life, and beyond.

I was startled to discover the old men felt compassion for me, still having to deal with emotion and thought. They encouraged me to live by heart-feelings instead. A different perspective.

Sometimes, when a young man goes on a fast, he practically demands a vision. The old men beg for compassion that their sacrifice might benefit the people. It is a different perspective.

We each learn about Fire and Stone: In our own ways, we learn about Light and consciousness. The difference between paths is perspective (the direction we view from), and the hue of consciousness (medicine powers). It is still all consciousness and Light.

The difference between Native ways and Christianity, or Shinto, is perspective. The underlying fundaments of human consciousness and perception are the gutrock underlying all religious ways. They are the Stone Dreams.

The Fire Teachings are a way through the manifest to live a good life in heart-warmth and Light, slowly uncovering spiritual ability as we grow through the years. Everything is perception and the levels of consciousness. The opening of awareness is to generate Light.

We should recall that the medicines are an aid. When we see a traditional person who carries a hawk wing fan, we can safely assume that he knows something of hawk medicine. The sacred objects tell us about the medicine ways of a person. These are things that help the person to change perceptions and consciousness, to draw closer to ethereal awareness.

I see non-natives carrying an owl wing fan. They get one somewhere and just start using it. They buy a drum and try to conduct ceremony in sweats. They tell people that they apprenticed for two years with a medicine man and that they are now also a medicine man. There is no apprenticeship as the white word means.

A man has a vision or an experience and might seek the guidance and advice of older, more experienced people. Once in a while, one has a vision of someone they should help for a while. I have walked up to complete strangers and handed them an eagle feather because of visions. They always say what I said when I got my first feather "How did you know to give it to me? Where did this feather come from exactly?"

When non-natives attend a sweat and then think they can now conduct ceremony it is just silly. There is this proprietary attitude towards Native things. One would not think of dressing up like the Pope, making a staff and robes like his, and leading an Easter Mass. Yet people buy Native things and think this qualifies them to conduct ceremony.

People of this time are seeking, and have to start somewhere. I will tell you something. I had a sweat with several young men. During the sweat, two owls landed above the lodge and began hooting and screeching. As I was in ceremonial consciousness, I understood them. They said that two old men very close to me were going to die soon. I asked who, and they said one was Uncle Mark. They told me that he knew already, and chose to die. The other old man was my paternal grandfather. He was in his nineties but very fit. I asked what could be done to keep them here. The owls said, "Nothing." I asked about fasting, Sundance, ceremony, offerings, and much more. The owls said nothing would help. I was being told so I would prepare. Finally, in desperation, I started to think of unorthodox things that were still in keeping with the Whole.

I asked if the owls could take their place. The Grandfathers who were talking to me through the physical owls were shocked. They thought I meant them. I clarified it, saying the physical owls could volunteer to take their place, and for this go completely into the spirit realm.

After a moment, the Grandfathers said that one owl would take my grandfather's place, but that Uncle Mark was definitely going and chose to go in this manner. The physical owl then spoke, saying, "When you find my body in the morning, you will know that it is so."

The Grandfathers said my own grandfather was going to have a major stroke, and would still have it. But he would survive.

The next morning we got up early to go to a reservation about a hundred miles away. Just after starting off I spotted a dead owl on the side of the road. Not one feather was ruffled, and there were no wounds of any kind. The body was warm, despite the early morning dew everywhere else. It looked like it just lay down and died. It had died just moments before we found it. I gave tobacco and prayed. Then I asked if I would be allowed to take any parts of the body for ceremonial use. I would never assume, even after the powerful events, that I could just do what I wanted. I was shown what to take, and made my fan from the tail feathers. The tail gives stability to a bird in flight. This is how I came to use an owl tail fan in ceremony. I did not just shoot an owl and make a fan. That would not be right.

I was living with Fools Crow when Uncle Mark died. We went to his wake together. Shortly after that, I got word that my grandfather had a major stroke and was not expected to live. He could not move, spit ran down his chin, and he lost all his English. I told Fools Crow, and after a brief consultation I informed him that I was going to sweat. He gravely nodded assent. In the sweat, just after I started praying for my grandfather, I saw a vision of the owls above my own sweat. I knew my grandfather would be okay, no matter what the physicians said.

Two weeks later, he was walking, talking, and doing his gardening. The physicians said it was a medical miracle. I knew better. It was the owls and the Grandfathers.

But, like I said, I do not have any things any more. I have no Pipe, drum, rattles, buffalo horn dippers, or fans. Bad medicine people tried to put curses on them, and so-called chiefs even tried to steal them. They thought they could get power from them. I loaned my fan to a hereditary chief once, and he said it was so good he was just keeping it. He refused to return it, and I had to barge into his bedroom and demand it back. I had trusted him until then.

When I accepted Fools Crow's invitation to come live with him for four seasons, his stepson told me: "Some bad people are jealous of the old man. They want to sell mining leases and make money off tribal land, and he won't let them ruin the land. They can't hurt him because he is too powerful. But if you stay here, they might take it out on you. You might end up crippled, or even dead." There are some bad people around.

I will tell you about this bad medicine. It is when someone else imposes a consciousness, or perception, on you. It may be the consciousness of a dying person, and then you are ill. They mess with your awareness, feelings, energy. They might only know that in the spirit realm they make medicine against you. But this is what it boils down to.

To combat bad medicine, you must realize that it is a consciousness put *on* you; it is not *in* you.

You must reach deep into inner consciousness and centering to simply throw it off you. It is not easy, but this can be done. It is like having a foul, smelly blanket thrown over you. If you give in to it, it wears you down. If you can throw it off, the fresh air soon revives you.

You could be made to perceive that countless powerful enemies are about to corner you. This has been done to some people to make them leave the rez.

You must have a fundamental consciousness to reach to. A strong belief is not enough. It must be a truth of existence. If you cannot do this, use conventional medicine ways or seek aid from a Holy One.

When I stayed with Grandpa Fools Crow, people came from other states and countries for help. Some came from Germany, Austria, France, Italy, and even Japan. They had heard of his honest reputation.

Every family used to keep herbs on hand, but sought help for major problems by consulting Holy Men.

We each will encounter our own medicines if we follow the Native way. We will be fascinated by them for a time. We will encounter different levels of consciousness, and be absorbed by the content rather than the nature of the experience. Eventually we become more stable in spiritual awareness and might even go beyond the need of rituals.

We should recognize the overall pattern because one day it can be fulfilled in us. It is normal in the Native way to use these things. But, newcomers do not seem to understand that we can get beyond them. It is a stage of learning. It is true that not all native people are called to go all the way. This is the same in any Way. But we should know the possibility exists.

As I said, thirty years is about the shortest time it takes to understand Native ways. It might take some fifty or sixty years. At that time, a person might slowly begin the process of assembling their medicine wheel. This can take quite a while. This means taking all of their knowledge and experiences and making a coherent understanding of life, Spirit, and Light. So, when non-natives in their twenties say that they are putting together their inner medicine wheel, they are mistaken. They have found their body center, which leads them to the outer circle of harmony of the wheel. They have not yet encountered the spokes, or the central cairn.

Generally, it is after this minimum thirty-year learning that someone can begin to really stabilize spiritual awareness. It might happen intermittently before then that they do not need ritualistic ceremony. In the Christian way, this happens soon. There are few things in what Jesus taught that could be considered ritualistic at all. Jesus enacted truths. He did not teach a set of traditional rituals. To heal a man of blindness, He spit on some soil and rubbed it on the man's eyes. Then He told the man to wash in a certain fountain. This is an enactment based upon knowledge of the spiritual meanings. It was ceremonial consciousness, but not a ceremony per se.

I was taught that in the way of Jesus, it takes about twenty years to learn about life, Light, and Spirit. The wondrous thing about Jesus as a man is that practically on the day He finished His twenty-year walk, He began to prepare for His death. He allowed Himself to be killed to accomplish His work. He had started His walk when He went to Jerusalem and talked to the elders.

I will talk about His first public miracle. When He turned water into wine, why did He not just make it so? He instructed the servers to fill Stone pots with water. When they tasted it, it was the finest wine. What makes this *enactment* is that when the waters of fluid one-ness and wholeness are placed into the receptacle of fundamental perception, the wine of the ability to transcend is the result. This is why Jesus did not just make it so—because He wished to demonstrate ceremonial enactment inherent with ethereal meaning.

Having learned Native ways since childhood, I cannot help but notice that in the Biblical story there were six Stone pots, corresponding to the four directions and the above and below realms. These are the six Grandfathers we speak of. Each Grandfather represents mastery over one direction.

This is an enactment of cosmic meaning. It is a ceremonial enactment, but churches have tried to make a ritual of it anyway, related to the Last Supper. They say that the wine is turned into the blood of Jesus during Mass. The symbol should be water turned to wine. Churches may get drunk on the wine, but not go beyond. They do not teach transcendence.

You see, Jesus was also a man with a manifest body. Like every human being,

He had to balance the physical and ethereal realms. This is centering. He was born with raised consciousness but still had the body realm to deal with. As a man He fasted alone, prayed, and sought development.

He did not come to erase sins from the world. He taught how we could be accepted back into Spirit and sin no more.

He taught enlightenment and the use of mystic consciousness. But He has been made into an unapproachable god-thing that we can only fear or marvel at. By doing this to Jesus the man, churches have effectively blocked us from ever daring to finish our learnings and be on the same level as the teacher. This is exactly opposite of what He taught.

Jesus bled when wounded. He ate. And He went to the bathroom. He had a normal body, born of woman.

I have told you that I had a vision when I was young. I was dying and went to a mountaintop. Someone came and talked to me. It was Jesus.

The Jesus in my vision had darkish hair, and a strong straight nose. He had a beard. The authority about Him was not to be mistaken. I wanted to revere Him, but He would not let me. He said that was not why He came into flesh. I asked many questions, and received answers.

I asked what His life was really all about. He said that He came to teach the world that people could transcend. So He was born with a physical side to deal with. He said it was fore-ordained that the world would not understand. This necessitated His return. I asked when that would be, and He said, "Soon." (In spiritual time, soon can be a hundred years.)

He said that when He returns, it will not be like anything anyone could imagine, not even mystics. I asked Him, if He was born in flesh, and was so holy, what was His true nature then?

As a reply, He changed consciousness. His face began to glow, then radiate the brightest white Light I could imagine, and then brighter than I could imagine. I had to turn away, not because of physical brilliance, but because of the purity of Spirit it represented. The Light grew until it obscured His body, and that is when I turned away. I knew when it stopped, because I could feel the changing consciousness.

To understand this properly took me about twenty years. It was not until I flew as a sphere of Light myself, that I could begin to understand this. When we fly as spheres of Light, the color of Light and hues of those colors indicates the level and kind of awareness we have. It reflects the nature of our learning way. If a sphere is mostly scarlet, it can mean the man is one of great powers like the intensity of fire. For Jesus to be pure white Light means that His consciousness and devotion to Spirit are the purest there can be, and the one-ness He reached with Spirit is perfect.

For Jesus to transfigure in the body realm into His Light-self bespeaks of unimaginable power. While He was in body, the two realms were fully as one to

Him. It is not that He could dwell at the center of the two realms, but was always in both at the same time. He was completely aware from the body.

I have seen powerful things through the years, but this boggles my mind. It is as far beyond flying as a sphere of Light, as we might think flying as a sphere is beyond the physical. I believe this is how He came back into body life. The power would be sufficient to burn His image into a burial shroud. I had never heard of the Shroud of Turin when I was twelve, but the Jesus in my vision looked just like pictures I later saw of the shroud. The power would be enough to baffle any scientific tests we could devise.

I asked Jesus if He ever appeared to people in daily life. He said never. But He said that He does meet people at the top of the mountain. He said that He talks to people, and they go back down from the mountain.

In later years, after going to the center, I understood this symbology. The top of the mountain is the highest we can go while maintaining touch with body life. When old Native people are getting ready to die, they say they are climbing the mountain. This means that they are getting less aware in the physical, and more aware of the spirit realm. It means that people with near-death experience are symbolically atop the mountain, and there meet Jesus. I believe those accounts because I was dying of pneumonia when I had my vision.

In my own vision, it was Jesus who taught me how to go beyond the top of the mountain, and more importantly, how to return.

I traveled to the upper level of clouds. There, I found a council of elders. They asked me how I came to be there, and why I was there. I told them that Jesus told me how to get there, and they were immensely pleased. I asked them, If they were Native elders, why were they so happy about Jesus? They said that only Jesus enters the spirit realm through the East. This is also in the Bible.

Through His life, He earned a unique place in the cosmos, they said. Each Way has a realm in the spirit worlds for its followers to go to.

Jesus also said He was preparing a room in the Father's house for His followers. Native peoples have a room, Buddhists have a room.

One thing that impressed me, but which I readily accepted, was that Jesus said His followers are His brothers and sisters in Light, not lesser subjects. He is still the Master with authority, but we may become as Masters ourselves. Later, I found this in the Bible.

We are children of the same Light. Therefore, we are equal in that. In His walk as a man, Jesus did not use ritual to heal. He did, however, use ceremonial enactments. These were based upon symbolic cosmic meaning.

If you follow this type of learning, you might use enactments. Jesus' way is more involved with enlightenments, transcendences, and changing consciousness. The Native way is involved with the same things, but more through ritual and use of nature. You see, the directions are even in the Bible: the "Queen of the South," the "Star of the East." There are a lot of symbolic enactments told in the Bible.

But in that way they are not the main thing. They are not a central theme. They are just a known side issue. Even though Native ways use symbols and ceremonial ritual a lot, it is known that these things are aids along the way and that we might transcend their use.

Spiritual development is the only thing. This deals in perception and consciousness. We will encounter symbolic meanings of all things, if we go to the center. For this reason, I say that no one way is the path, or the way.

Yours might be real to you, but there is no one and only religion. Any religion could disappear from the earth. The Light would always exist for people to find.

NINE

HEALING IS ACCOMPLISHED BY DISCOVERING YOUR PROPER FLOW WITHIN THE LARGER PATTERN.

The first time that I went to the reservation where Uncle Mark lived was in response to a visionary seeing. I saw that if I drove to the rez, the first man that I talked to would take me to ceremonial sweatlodge right away. When my heart felt the time was right, I got into my old blue pick-up truck and started driving. The three days that I drove, wave after wave of energy kept passing through me, cleansing me. When I reached the border of the rez on the third day, I stopped and prayed. I asked for spiritual protection while I was there. I heard an old man say that I would be watched over, and wondered who he was. I inwardly saw a very old man sitting in an armchair under a tree, and where he lived. I knew that I would meet him in several years. It was Grandfather Fools Crow.

As I drove through the rez, I knew that if I stopped my truck at the Bureau of Indian Affairs (BIA) offices, the man I was to meet would walk right up to my truck. I parked and waited. Then I heard the man telling me that he was delayed, and that if I went to the next town, he would catch up to me soon.

This was not as I had seen; so I drove out of town and offered tobacco. I asked for a sign that this was the right thing to do.

Just as I started driving again, a great bird suddenly swooped over the cab of my truck and flew at eye-level ahead of me. It was an eagle. I had never seen a golden eagle before, having been raised in the East. His wingspan seemed to cover one whole lane of the road. He glided ahead of me for about three hundred feet, and then banked. Slowly, he beat his great wings to climb higher. Directly over a housing project he began to circle. This was where the man lived.

As I stepped out of my truck, a woman was getting out of a station wagon with several young boys. She turned to me and said, "Oh, there you are. Can you watch the kids a while? My husband is delayed at the BIA."

Native women never trust strangers with their children. I looked at her a moment, and said, "Sure."

She blinked, and really looked at me, then. She realized that she did not know me, and yet had asked me to safeguard the most precious thing. When her husband arrived, she told him what had happened and he talked to me. Within moments, he said that he was going to a sweat that evening and that he could take me along. He said that we should leave in a few minutes to get wood and prepare for the sweat. Then we sat there over two hours. I realized he was testing my patience, and simply went off somewhere inside myself. Finally, he sighed and said, "Let's go, then."

As we were cutting dead trees for the sweat fire, we did not talk. A pheasant wandered through the dry stream bed, and stopped a moment. With a gesture of his head, the man indicated the bird.

"You know what that is?" he asked.

"Yeah, pheasant," I said.

"Nope. White man medicine. Their European animals are replacing ours. It doesn't belong here. It came from Europe, or from somewhere else, probably. This was the last land with its own animals."

That single pheasant summed up everything to this man: the loss of the wild, free life; the loss of traveling with tipi and greeting the sun each morning; the loss of being at home wherever you traveled because you were always at the center of all you perceived; the replacement of Native ways with Christianity and capitalism. That bird said it all: pollution, destruction of the natural environment, brain-washing at boarding schools, fear of Native religion and language as evil witchcraft, life in tenement housing with bad water, bad insulation, sickness, and confinement to one piece of land. That one stupid pheasant, too dumb to run when it saw us, summed it up for that man. He looked as though he would like to wring its neck, but he shrugged and said, "It is here, now."

We cut the wood for the fire, cleaned the lodge, and selected the stones—all in silence. As he was passing used stones out from the lodge-pit, he suddenly yelled at me harshly, "If you can't do things right, leave."

I looked at the stone in my hand, looked at him, and simply kept on as before.

I was being tested again for emotional reaction. I simply kept on as before.

When we had everything ready, he sat looking at me. After about fifteen minutes, he said, "A lot of people come from all over for this. Damned few get in the lodge. Some white people come, even Indians from northern Canada. We don't let them in. You are getting in. You should know it is not common."

"I know."

"This is the real thing tonight."

I asked him what happened in the lodge, and told him that I knew absolutely nothing about it. He said that I would find out. To know that, I would have to go in the lodge.

The Pipe Carrier who would lead the rite arrived. When he saw me, he was puzzled. He knew there would be a guest that night, but he remarked that something was "watching over that boy." (Anyone under forty is called a boy.)

When the stones were brought in, white hot, and blessed, the entry flap was closed and we were in total darkness. You could not see your own hand an inch before your eyes.

In the lodge, I heard four earth-shaking steps of stately dignity, and an ancient buffalo walked into the lodge. He was like a full-sized buffalo, but somehow walked into the lodge. He walked to me, and snorted in my ear. Then, with four more earth-shaking steps, he left. In the next round, the whole lodge lit up inside like strong moonlight, and we could see each other clearly. In the third round, I suddenly could no longer hear the singing or feel the intense steam. I reached down to steady myself, but I could not touch the ground. Hard-packed soil was directly under me, but as I sat cross-legged and reached down as far as I could, I could not touch the earth. I did not know if I was floating or had become insubstantial. In the fourth round, I had a series of visions relating to my role in Native religion.

This was my first ceremonial sweat.

It was not run by a man of great powers, just a Pipe Carrier who had done everything properly. I have heard of a lot of non-natives who read a book and then made a lodge. They complain that they do not have visions in the lodge. Some say that after knowing Native people for ten years, they feel they have not gotten very far. Well, it takes at least thirty years to get anywhere. It is more than reading one book. It is for life.

When we left the lodge and had poured sage-water over our bodies to rinse off the sweat, I began to wonder at what had really happened here.

I stared at the fire pit where we had heated the stones all afternoon. I looked at the altar of mellowed earth, and at the shape of the lodge. I gazed at the shallow pit that held the now-cooling stones in the center of the lodge. I saw the bucket the cool water had been in. I looked back and forth between these several times, and knew what had happened. By the time I looked around again, everyone had left but the man who had brought me. He was staring at me intently, probably wondering what I was so absorbed in. Since neither of us had eaten all day, and it was almost midnight, he invited me back to his house for a meal.

Back at the housing project, he scrounged some leftovers and threw together a meal. As we ate, he explained that some people came seeking ceremony, and they found only the physical sweat run by those who were not even medicine men. Some had come to the rez for years but had never been to a real ceremony. Some fell in with those who wanted dogs.

Some years later, I was invited to a sunrise sweat by a friend. As we heated the stones, my friend saw me preparing myself and came over.

"This is just a sweat," he said, "not a ceremony. I just want to give some white friends a taste of the real thing." To me, this is wrong. If you want people to know what a real sweat is like, have a real sweat. A watered-down version is not a sweat; it is just a sauna.

Many years later, my own father was dying of cancer. I had seen that he would die, but not exactly how. I prayed and made ceremony, but could not do anything. My father was resolved to die, so his spirit stubbornly refused that his body be healed. I thought maybe my friend the grizzly-dreamer might be able to help. I prayed that the Spirits guide us both, and was told what to take him.

When I arrived at the grizzly-dreamer's reservation, he greeted me at the door of his house: "You can't stay today! The Spirits told me someone is bringing a loaded Pipe." (Someone in grave need might bring a Pipe already filled on behalf of someone who cannot make the journey themselves because of illness.)

I reached into the paper sack and took out the filled Pipe I had brought. His eyes went wide for a second, but he merely grunted in bear fashion and took the Pipe into his bedroom. In a moment, he called me to join him and we smoked the Pipe. When I told him the problem, he said he had been heating stones for sweat all day, and that a mutual friend would come to be the door-man (someone who passes in the stones and water, and closes and opens the entry flap).

Once in the sweat, he sang his bear songs and I prayed. He confirmed that because my father had firmly resolved to die at this time, nothing could be done. To overrule his free choice and keep him here forcibly would be an infringement against his spirit, and a grave wrong. I had to just let him go.

Then my friend said the Spirits wanted to use the rattle. He placed the rattle beside me, and moved to the back of the lodge. He began to sing again, and I heard the rattle being lifted gently. It began to shake and with each movement light green sparks of intense light played over its surface. They flew off into the darkness a little ways. The rattle circled the lodge and then began to doctor me with gentle blows against my body. There is no way to describe what I felt with each blow. I heard my friend singing in the back of the lodge, but needed no confirmation that he had not moved. I believe in the Spirits. The rattle suddenly was gone, but moments later returned and circled the lodge once before setting itself down beside me again. My friend said the Spirits had taken the rattle to the hospital where my father lay dying, and prepared him for death. The Spirits got him into a better consciousness and "took him up the mountain."

After the sweat, my friend gave me almost a gallon of herbal tea used for cancer. We both knew my father would not take it. My father chose to go, and refused all help. Every person deserves the right to die in the manner they choose.

After the Spirits prepared my father, he began to talk in the Indian way for the first time. He was on top of the mountain now, and could communicate telepathically. I had a long talk with him in this way the night he died. He sent me away at the end, to be alone. About two hours later, he died.

Often, when you bless the stones as they go into the central pit of the lodge, a light blue neon light spreads over their surface, and then shoots into the very heart of each stone, pulsing gently there. The first time I conducted a ceremonial sweat, the light was a pale green color, but after that it was blue.

I built my lodge on the site of an old Native village on a bluff above a river. I did not know this at first. No one has yet discovered the old site, and I was led to it by a sphere of blue light. It floated gently before me through a woods. Where it hovered, and then disappeared as I arrived, was a perfect circle of young pine trees. The circle opened to the West, my direction. Directly beyond this opening is a huge ancient cedar tree. The perfect place for a ceremonial sweat. It was here that I talked with the owls for the first time.

You can find dozens of books telling how to build the physical lodge. I would like to talk about other parts of it. One woman I met recently said she feared sexuality at a sweat because men and women are practically naked. This is wrong. In the way I was taught, men wear short pants or the equivalent. Men also wear a T-shirt if there are women present who are not direct family. Women wear a loose cotton dress that covers the knees.

In the real old way, men and women do not sweat together. Other nations have their own ways. A Lakota man may sweat with his wife, or young female relatives who have not reached puberty. Otherwise, men and women do not sweat together. If a medicine man must sweat with a woman to help her, both parties must insist on at least one older woman as chaperone, preferably several.

Nowadays, people are losing this respect, the affording of dignity to each other. I follow Uncle Mark's way. He did not sweat with women unless doctoring them. If you sing the Pipe song in the right way, everyone feels like brothers and sisters at ceremony. You do not think sexually about a sister.

If I make ceremonial sweatlodge, I insist on doing all the preparations myself. I quarry the sandstone, cut the wood, clean the lodge, prepare and watch the fire. If a special purpose has been called, such as the request of someone for a special sweat, I make over four hundred tobacco offerings strung together. These are tobacco ties—a pinch of tobacco or pipe mixture tied into a tiny pouch, and all the pouches strung together in a continuous line. It takes hours to do this.

The four rounds of sweatlodge reflect the four directions, four levels of a whole self, four stages of human growth, and the four parts of the Fire Teachings.

The principles of sweatlodge are these: The lodge itself is shaped like the dome of the heavens. It represents the limitations of mortal perception. We live our lives under that dome, in the darkness of unknowing. We cannot see beyond it into the ethereal. Under this dome, in spiritual darkness, we seek Light and to go beyond the limitations. Sometimes the lodge will light up inside. Sometimes the top of the lodge falls away and there is no lodge above you. The night sky beyond is revealed. This reflects that you have transcended. But the contents of the experience often distract from understanding the nature of the experience.

The workings of a ceremonial sweat are these: Trees provide us with the fuel for the fire. We each have something similar in us. Trees are called the Standing People. Like the trees, we are rooted in the physical. We reach upward as they do. We reach for the rain of spiritual blessing, and for Light. Through this material-life way, and seeking, we find the ability to focus and concentrate ourselves. This is the intensity needed to transcend. It is the latent intensity found in dead wood. We begin to gather the dead wood for a sweat fire. We are gathering our focus at the same time, thinking and feeling what is to come in the lodge. We are changing our mood and feelings. This wood is used to heat up the stones. Our intensity is used to change consciousness.

By changing perceptions, through changing our mood and feeling as we prepare for the lodge, we are speeding and elevating consciousness. As the stones begin to heat up, they begin to glow: first red, and then white.

Their particles vibrate at a faster speed. This produces Light, first the intensity of red-hot stone, and then the brilliance of white-hot stone. This is the change that we seek in our selves. First comes the intensity, then the harmony. Both are Light.

In the lodge, we place the stones one at a time into the shallow central pit. We invite blessing of the stones as we sprinkle sacred herbs on them. The stones are placed to symbolize the directions, which represent the four levels of self. By inviting blessing of the stones, we are inviting the same changes to occur in us, as symbolized by the white-hot stones. We also are expressing that we wish this to be a spiritual experience, and so we invite blessing.

In the lodge we center ourselves around this central theme. When we are all prepared, the one conducting the rite knows. Then he calls for the entry-way to be closed, and we are sealed into utter darkness. For a while, the stones glow and illuminate the darkness, and we center ourselves in this more and more. After an invocation, the prayer and sacred songs begin. Cool water is splashed on the stones, and the steam hisses and spits. This act is sometimes said to symbolize our prayers rising like the steam. I prefer to say it symbolizes the fluid one-ness of things and that this is the perception that elevates us once we have speeded consciousness. *We* are lifted like the steam, not just our prayers. These are fundaments of sweatlodge.

The soil removed to make the shallow central pit for the heated stones is broken up finely. Roots and stones are removed, and this softened soil is made into a round mound about three feet before the lodge door, between the lodge and the fire pit. This is mellowed earth, the altar upon which we rest the Pipe and all sacred things. This is the primal Lodge ceremony.

The Pipe is not necessary for sweatlodge. It is customary to use it, but not crucial. A buffalo skull is not crucial. Many people have become more absorbed in visionary content, rather than the transcendent nature of the ceremony. When sweatlodge is conducted only in the physical, it is physical renewal like any sauna. You will notice the body changes that intense heat and steam will produce. That is all. When sweatlodge is conducted as a transcendent ceremony, everyone will change consciousness. It can be quite dramatic.

It is said that if you sweat with a man of power, great things can happen, strong things. What is really meant by the word power is the facility to change fundamental perceptions and consciousness. When you attend ceremony conducted by a powerful man, or Vision Quest with his help, you will have a strong experience. By strong we also mean fundamental.

If someone lives with a strong heart, it is fundamental heart, fundamental deep feeling, not surface emotions.

Sometimes when people fast this way, miraculous things happen. Some men fast near each other for solace and comfort through the long cold nights.

Sometimes, in late afternoon as night approaches, a man will suddenly disappear All his sacred things are gone, too. From one second to the next, they are just gone. In the morning, after sun-up, he is suddenly just back again. We say the Spirits took him somewhere to teach him. It might be somewhere else in this world, or the spirit world.

Power is almost inconceivable to mortals who have not pierced the dome, or the veil separating the worlds. I know of one butte that a power man actually moved. He was having ceremony, and said that because of all the nearby mining and agriculture, the flow around the butte was slightly off. The butte was a long narrow one running exactly west-east. Everything went very swimmy during the ceremony, and then the butte was sitting northwest by southeast. It stayed that way. I can only tell you what I personally know to be true, because I witnessed it.

I have also seen objects moved over great distance, and in one case, also through time. Just the fact that I was taught all this by six voices that turned out to be living, flesh-and-blood mystics speaks of untold powers. Not *my* powers, but that Power with a capital "P."

I was raised Catholic Christian, and was even an altar boy for eleven years, while at the same time being taught the old Native ways. I asked the priests about Moses, and Abraham, and the voices they heard. The priests said that people back then were less sophisticated, and less technologically minded. They implied that only stupid, undeveloped people could think they heard voices. They implied that only very simple people could talk over distance telepathically, and have mystical experiences, or think they did. Some attitudes are changing now, some for the better, others for the worse. But, I think I will stay less technologically minded.

When I received my long-stemmed ceremonial Pipe, I was very devoted. I smoked it at least once a day, making ceremony even if all alone. I liked to go to natural areas a lot and found that I preferred a deserted gravel pit where many of the herbs I used still grew.

One day, after centering myself through gesturing the directions, I sat on the edge of a bluff overlooking a river. Behind me was the gravel pit and the herb field. Beside me a small stream cascaded in a series of waterfalls to the river sixty feet below. As I let myself merge with the one-ness of all things, a small head poked over the lip of the bluff. A forked tongue flicked at me, and a snake about a yard long slithered over the edge. I never liked snakes. It came to where I sat cross-legged, and curled up against my thigh. The snake rested its head on its coils and seemed to doze. I went back to what I had been doing. When I finished, I thanked the snake for teaching me trust. It bobbed its head as I slowly stood, and it calmly slithered back over the edge of the bluff.

Another time, in another part of the herb field, I sat on a small rise of land and made ceremony. It was about four in the afternoon. As I prayed, I noted that birds often came to me during ceremony, but usually not mammals. I asked if there was any particular reason mammals did not seem to attend my ceremonies.

I bent forward and lowered my head over my Pipe as I prayed, closing my eyes for a moment. When I looked up, a red fox stepped from behind a hillock. It began to calmly hunt crickets and mice, about sixty feet from me. It leaped high into the air, pouncing on intended prey. I watched it hunt for a few moments, and called out in a loud voice. I thanked it for coming to my Pipe. The fox stopped, and looked all around. It seemed not to see me.

It resumed hunting, and I sang a sacred song, loudly. It seemed not to notice in the least. I prayed, and the fox wandered part of the herb field hunting. I called out to it once more, at the end of my Pipe, thanking it for showing me there was no reason for mammals not to come to my ceremonies. I cleaned the bowl of my Pipe, and gently separated the bowl from the stem. In that split second, the fox whipped its head around and saw me. Within half a moment, it was a red dot at the edge of the distant woods.

During ceremony I had been inseparable from the rest of the Spirit in all things. I later learned to use this to stay unnoticed by passers-by when I did not want interruptions. There are powerful and mysterious things.

When I was sixteen, after I had accepted to continue the learnings, I was granted some looks into the future before setting aside all I had learned. I saw many things to be, including a marriage, and a woman whom I would meet when I left the rez. I saw the men who would wish me ill, and those who would be relatives. I saw what the first two old men would try to do to me, and I immediately began to lament and mourn. Suddenly, I heard a new group of people talking to me over distance. Until now, my teachers had prevented anyone from listening in on our talks. Obviously, this now was opened up.

"Who are you? Why are you sad? How can we reach you? Who is hurting you that you mourn so sad?"

I said to them, in symbolic language, "They tied my hands and my feet and they threw me in the River. I can't get out! I am drowning!"

Many years later, I discovered that one part of this group was in a sweatlodge near where Uncle Mark lived. They were organizing physical search parties to drag the river by the sweat, thinking this was the spirit of a missing youth talking. A medicine man looked into it, and told them not to do that. I was not drowned in any physical river.

One of the women who talked to me, talked with me again the next day. When I described how difficult it was living among the dominant society, and yet knowing the old ways, she said she would adopt me as her son in the Lakota way. She would be my Lakota mother. She said, "This summer when you visit the old man, I will camp next to you at the big powwow, and then we will start to be relatives."

I told her that I was not where she was, and this was strange to me. She did not understand. I had no words to tell her that I knew she was speaking and hearing me twelve years in my future. I knew that my position in time and space was different than hers.

The woman turned out to be Fools Crow's daughter, Marie, and twelve years later I camped next to her. She treated me as a beloved son. I could not bring myself to talk to anyone about this time-talking that happened, and never have. I could accept that I talked to people far away—but through time as well? I made up my mind that one of the tasks I would set myself would be to understand this, if possible, one day.

This time-talking has happened several times. I conversed with someone over distance, and knew their time and location in space. Only one man seemed aware of this ability, but I never discussed it with him. It is something so abstract that if you know, you know. If you do not, words will not help much.

I saw Grandpa Fools Crow do an old-time ceremony once. A woman came who was ill, and the non-native doctors could not help her except to treat symptoms with pain pills. Grandpa had told me that we would be driving to Rapid City that day. But early in the morning he told me we had to wait, as someone was now coming for help. When the woman arrived, Grandpa made ceremony. During this, he took a single eagle feather and brushed her down. Then, he tapped the feather against a bowl and a live caterpillar fell out of the end of the feather. He asked me to burn it up.

He said this was what someone put in her to make her ill. It was the bad medicine. I do not believe the actual caterpillar was in her. I believe that the bad medicine was taken out of her and made into a caterpillar.

The ability to use powers, have visions, be in ceremonial consciousness, is a fundamental perception. It is taught to us through learned people, or through spiritual guidance.

By feeling the mood of the learned ones, we begin to sense what that consciousness is like. It begins with mood and feelings. Telling of experiences is meant to help us capture the feeling for ourselves. I have written as I have to avoid one mood that everyone seems to write about. You should know that there is more than one kind of consciousness or perception; there is more than one hue.

In my life I have witnessed many things. I have wept in joy at the beauty before me, and laughed in joy at life's simplest things many people take for granted. I tell my experiences, but not what I felt. When you have experiences, your heart will sing. When you participate with the Spirit in all things, you have a certain attitude and consciousness. The fairness of life becomes clear to you. Life is fair; we have just forgotten the rules.

A right, or good act is one which is in accord with the Holy Spirit in all things. To be able to know that movement, and therefore what is whole and complete, we must arrive at inner balance. This comes through the Fire Teachings.

Wrong acts, or evil acts, are those contrary to the wholeness of the Spirit in all things. Even in the Bible, this is what is meant by the Original sin. Adam and Eve were without shame, and were told to be fruitful and multiply. Sex is certainly not a sin. Adam and Eve were diligently practicing being fruitful before they ate the fruit of the tree of knowledge. Rather, the tree reveals what is good and what is evil. It is knowledge of right and wrong. If everything was created by the Creator and only He existed, then creation came into being as a manifestation of the Creator's intent. This is the Spirit in all things, the Creator within His creation. If everything is perceived as manifestation of the Creator, and imbued with Spirit, there can be no perception of a right or wrong act because everything is within the movements of the Spirit in all things—Holy Spirit.

In other words, before eating the fruit, humankind could not perceive right from wrong because everything was within the Holy Spirit in all things, and therefore only good could perceived. When people ate the Biblical fruit, and could therefore perceive right from wrong, they committed the Original sin of removing themselves from the flowing Holy Spirit in all things. They discovered isolation and ego, for they suddenly became embarrassed for the first time because they were naked.

In using power, we follow the flowing movements of the sacred Spirit in all things. From understanding the actions and movements of the ethereal breath of God, we understand something moving in us as well. Against this spiritual movement, we will weigh our own acts and motivations while slowly growing more whole and complete. If these are within the patterns and flowing one-ness, they are proper acts.

For this reason, when we are doctoring someone, we can see the illness as an intrusion or interruption in the flowing movements of a person. We can tell where the discord lies, and assess how best to correct it. We can do this, because we understand how the flow should be.

This wholistic approach is used the world over by natural people living with the land and with the Spirit in all things. By helping the person to achieve or to re-achieve their proper flowing within the larger pattern, healing is accomplished. As the body can grow ill from lack of nourishment or improper diet, so too can lack of, or improper, nourishment for the heart and soul cause us to be imbalanced or physically ill. Healing takes place from the spiritual realm. Before a physical healing can take place, the patient sometimes needs to draw closer to Spirit.

For all the adventures and mysterious happenings, nothing strikes me as important as balance, harmony, centering, generating Light. From the deepest center, we can emerge along any spoke of the wheel. All of these happenings are types of Stone in the great wheel. With repeated journeys to the center, we might begin to understand the nature of the medicine wheel, and our own life. We must get past our illusions and preconceived ideas.

TEN

WHEN YOU REACH HARMONY AND CAN LIVE THIS WAY WITH A GOOD, STRONG HEART, YOU HAVE REACHED A DEGREE OF HOLINESS AND LIGHT.

All of what I am doing in writing will be condemned by some. It may be said to be far too much intellectualization. It may be said to be off balance to spend so much time in intellect, and not in feeling and Spirit.

But, for this book, I must do this for a little while. I talk about fundamental consciousness, and the hues of consciousness. The fundaments are, of course, the principal levels of consciousness we may each have as human beings. Some of them are levels beyond manifestation. The hue of consciousness comes from your particular elemental character as reflected through the symbols and content of your medicine path. If a man learned through the use of powers, and intense fire demonstrations, his main color as a spirit of Light would be scarlet. This is hue.

If your medicine is of the deserts, it will have a different feeling and mood than that of deep woodlands. Each person learns to generate Light. Their personal way to arrive at this is reflected in the hue and color of their spiritual shining.

All of these things are just lived. Near the end of learnings, we can begin to understand the fundamental consciousnesses. Until then, we have but glimmerings of a far-off Light. Your vehicle of growth is to follow your own medicine way, whether that is elk medicine, bear, or Zen, or Jesus, or Shinto. You will feel affinity for your true way. It will not be forced. When we follow our own way, without worrying about what anyone else has or does, we live contented. These ways are but reflections of how an individual self interacts with Spirit. We follow our own way so that we may one day strip away all relative truths to uncover the absolute or true being. A way is a relative truth. You can transcend even your own way.

Not everyone will be the grand master-dreamer But the world needs chokecherry as much as it needs oak. Each does different things in the world, and produces different fruit. But each reaches upward to rain and light; each produces seed.

If you have reached harmony of Fire, you can more calmly determine action or re-action. You are rooted in harmony with the whole; so, interruptions to the flowing whole show up more clearly. Each of these elements of consciousness is symbolized by a Stone. Just as there are different feelings and character to hues of consciousness, there are different Stones symbolizing this in the stone altars. When you learn the fundamental consciousness that allows you to enter the mystic or cosmic wheel of life's realities, you will gradually notice changes. You learn one Stone, or state of consciousness, and gradually move on to the next. Learning the ways of harmony, you travel the outer circle of the wheel. To do this, you must seek your body center. This is the one Stone you start from. Some young non-natives who find the first Stone say they have put together their medicine wheel.

After learning the ways of harmony as you travel the outer circle of the wheel, you begin to travel in along the spokes. You begin to have mystical or spiritual experiences.

Eventually, through the decades of learning, we begin to comprehend more clearly. Some who first arrive at the center, still filled with illusion and impurity of mind, discover some spiritual power. They mistakenly think that it is all-encompassing. The individual sees something that is all that mind can encompass. They mistakenly think it is all there is in existence. No, you have only gone as far as mind can encompass. There are also heart and Spirit.

The fact that these people have not purified themselves keeps them from reaching ultimate power. Just as within the Native way there are hues to consciousness, different ways have their own sets of hues, or sacred perceptions. The fundamental consciousnesses are the same for all humanity. This makes them spiritual truths. A man from India might arrive at the golden-yellow Light but when he tells others, his frame of reference will be completely different. This is cultural influence. The Japanese Shintoist will use different thoughts for the same thing. South American Natives will say something else. Christians will say something different. It is all the same golden-yellow Light: It is a fundamental consciousness. We each followed our little spoke of the great wheel, carrying the impurities of cultural influence and context with us. Eventually, with purification, we begin to understand.

Each way has its own speeds of vibration. It is like a field of awareness and perception that we enter as we learn that way. Since I was also raised a Christian to some extent, I like to use that as my main comparison. Jesus said that the kingdom of heaven is all around us if we could but perceive it. I believe that He meant the Holy Spirit in all things, and the golden-yellow Light. If heaven is a place with streets and buildings covered in golden color, I think it must be entered through the golden Light of the center. The whole world, the very air is golden there.

If we could but change our speed of vibrations as we elevate consciousness, we could perceive this. The Bible also talks about the quick and the dead, which I like to interpret as the speeded up and the spiritually dead.

My own vision tells me that Native ways are a slow but safe ascent if you follow them purely. Along the way, we might encounter the pines and snow, trails of different medicine creatures.

At the same time, my vision tells me that Jesus stands atop a stone mountain bare of vegetation or creatures, and the sides of the mountain are sheer with no trails. In the future, things will be changing. But right now, this is how it has been.

Jesus says that if we follow His teachings, we will reach the same height as Him. There are no steps, no easy hand-holds to pull ourselves up those sheer cliffs. So today's Christians have not been able to do what Jesus said they could.

This will be changing.

What did Jesus do? He fasted, prayed, and spent as much time in natural areas and up mountains as He could. In the past, intense prayer rituals in Christianity could help some people to change consciousness. If you treat the Lord's Prayer as a meditation theme, you can begin to see the sense in it. Today, people are farther removed from the earth and the wholeness of living in accord with the physical environment. So it is harder to understand meditative prayer You may contemplate the prayer:

Our Father, who is in Heaven.
Our Creator, in the ethereal.

This places your consciousness on both the vast and powerful highest presence, and towards the ethereal heavenly realm. It is not just the Father of Jesus, but: *Our Father.*

If you wish to pray in the right way, seek the harmony and balance found in the Fire Teachings. How you arrive at that balance and harmony could be any one of thousands of ways.

Today, people are slowly realizing that Jesus did intend for His followers to grow spiritually. They just cannot find the connections. I have often heard people say that they would like to experience sweatlodge if they could do so and maintain their Christian context. People sense that they must open up somehow; they just do not yet know how to proceed.

Once you know the balance of the Fire Teachings you can proceed in any chosen way. With this harmony, you can fast and change consciousness. You can seek guiding visions and learn. To interpret your visions and experiences you might not find many who can put the experiences in Christian context. Perhaps, if you learn, you might one day be the old man who does this for the young people.

From this basis, you can seek in your own way. If you are truly drawn to Native ways, fine. If you are Christian, or follow Zen, fine. But seek.

If you can reach this harmony of perfect balance with the manifest world, you have created your mystical fasting circle. As you begin to learn more, you might even be called upon to experience the golden Light of the center. I refer to this as earning the mystical eagle feather.

This is to proceed from the manifest harmony of the Fire Teachings, to the spiritual harmony of being in the manifest and ethereal realms at the same time. This is why I say that everything starts with the Fire Teachings. After learning the harmony of the manifest realm, we can strive toward the ethereal spirit realm.

When you pray intensely in the Christian way you also bring about changes in perception. You make your body still because your devotion demands it. You slowly clear the mind through the repetition of the prayers. You begin to ponder the meanings and the impact of the words of the prayers. The love of the Father, and of Jesus, slowly fills you, and you feel your heart. This is the balance of the Fire Teachings.

These are the same elements as the Fire Teachings. You calm the body, clear the mind, feel your heart. You recognize Spirit as Light. All the same things are in Christianity as in the sacred Native ways of Fire and Stone. These are the elemental parts of human existence.

Some of the connections are just not easy to see. We have an incomplete picture because the Bible seems to take us from the twelve-year-old boy beginning His mystery walk, to the thirty-year-old mystic who is teaching. People wonder what happened to Him in between. Those who follow a mystical path can guess. He certainly spent a lot of time alone in wilderness, praying, fasting, and communing. He continued this while teaching and often went off alone away from the crowds, into wilderness areas and atop mountains.

Jesus said that He came to fulfill the scriptures (Old Testament). I prefer to interpret this as His having come to validate the scriptures.

Noah's flood can have happened in reality. Yet the symbolic meanings are as important as the literal fact. Great moments of spiritual truth always have both fact and meaning combined. This relates directly to Jesus' first miracle, and indirectly to the Last Supper.

I once spent four days fasting and praying for understanding of the Bible. I received just three verses, and their meanings. The passage of Noah drinking wine was the first. Jesus turning water into wine was the second. The third passage was that mankind lived in a state of grace (holiness) until knowing good from evil.

From these three verses, we can understand the whole Bible and its message.

These relate directly to what I have been saying about the Fire Teachings. The flood of Noah is to be flooded by the one-ness and wholeness of creation, and the meanings symbolized by all creatures. These are the creatures that he took with him. The waters symbolize the wholeness and one-ness that we can perceive. The flood also symbolizes an influx of this perception. The oceans are the waters to which all rivers and streams eventually flow. Ocean represents the one-ness that all spiritual seeking ways eventually reach. When Noah survived the flood he became a farmer and made wine. He went beyond ordinary body sensations. He went beyond mortal perception by transcending.

Jesus turned water into wine. This is comparable to saying that the balance of the Fire Teachings leads us toward transcending. The water is the harmony of Spirit found in perceiving the whole, the Spirit in all things. This perception becomes the ability to go beyond, to transcend, represented by the wine.

And this is how we return to the state of grace. This is how we return to the Great Spirit in all things, the Garden-of-Eden consciousness.

For me, these three passages explain the whole concept of the Bible and of spirituality. From this, we can begin to comprehend the rest of the Bible. What I have not yet talked about is a description of the hues of consciousness inherent to the various levels.

If you look around at the manifest world, you can see that people have differing views of themselves in relation to the world around them. This is what I call relativity. A plumber sees the world and his relation to it differently from a lawyer. They see it differently from a priest, who sees it differently from a prostitute. These might be said to be realities, or the dreams we have of ourselves and the world.

To uncover the real self, or inner self, is to realize what is but a dream, and also what is the underlying gutrock truth. This would be a fundamental perception: Stone Dreams.

If you take any one person as an example, there are multitudinous levels of reality and relativity in that person. The same person behaves differently when being the manager of a large company than when fishing with his boys. He is different alone with his wife and family. If that person were suddenly dropped into a totally unfamiliar context or environment, he would adapt to meet shifting circumstances. Stranded in the wilderness, his perception of the world and self in relation to it would change.

Somewhere, underlying the facets of self and how we view self in relation to the manifest world and other people, is the spiritual reality of inner self. Somewhere behind the dreams of self is the real self. Somewhere behind the shifting views of self is an inner, unchanging self. This is what we seek to know in the mystic search. This is what we call the center, the self at the very center of being. It is the calm, inner self around which our very lives swirl and change. In our search for this inner self, this balanced and whole self-awareness, we are drawn to differing ways that each have their own collective reality, or hue.

In the broader Native ways, this is recognized as being drawn to certain medicines as an individual. The person who has a vision of elk had those capacities in him before having the vision. The vision, or visionary dream, signifies the means by which the mortal being might draw closer to the spiritual side of being.

The hue of a way, or the spiritual medicine of a way, is partly a feeling and mood generated by that level of consciousness and the symbolic values of the visionary content. It is the nature of the elk-medicine that gives a hue or feeling to using elk-medicine consciousness. Since elk have something to do with sexual potency, the Fire is involved in elk medicine. The elk person will understand passion and emotional closeness.

The thunder-dreamer usually has a strong and sudden burst of spiritual energy dramatically making itself known, like the roaring thunder and crashing lightning. The wolverine has tenacity and single-mindedness of purpose. All the creatures and weathers give something towards the hue of a medicine way. The hues of spiritual awareness are partly accounted for by this. These medicines go toward the nature of a learning way. If a man's path is very concerned with revelations, he would fly as a yellow sphere of Light. If he was concerned with harmony, his sphere might be white. It may have another color with it. Some are a complete white, but liquid, not brilliant and mind-numbing.

All these ways reflect our connection between physical self and spiritual realization. They are earthly medicines that help us draw closer toward Spirit. Jesus also named (Mark 3:16-17) His disciples Stone (Peter), and Sons of Thunder (James and John). This has been largely overlooked by the churches.

Love and goodness are a part of spiritual medicines. When my teachers talked about having a good heart, they also meant everything you could think of as the teachings of Jesus about how to live right: Feed the hungry, clothe the naked, comfort the sick, have compassion for others. Every kind act that you could imagine is also what they meant. Live with a good heart toward other people and also toward all parts of creation.

When you reach harmony and can live this way with a good, strong heart, you have reached a degree of holiness and Light on whichever level you are on. You are in the Light, and it is a clear Light. It is white-based consciousness. It is harmony.

Wholeness and completeness are things you should be able to sense. To be complete is to somehow feel filled. Nothing is lacking. Nothing is craved. For me, the clearest association is that the wholeness of the natural world helps to foster within each of us this sense of wholeness. When body, heart, and mind are balanced, spiritual awareness is realized. Then we are whole.

When you feel whole and complete, you are living the balance of the Fire Teachings. It is the point at which you have reached awareness and balance of body, mind, and heart. At this time, you perceive the one-ness of the manifest world. You also perceive the one-ness of self. This opens the door for true spiritual awareness.

One reason to preserve the natural lands, aside from pure conservation, is to help foster within us this wholeness and one-ness. We go into nature to refresh and re-create our selves. Recreation is re-creation, to create again, create anew. When you live in this balance, the fire that you make in the woods is small. The fire inside you is smaller, too. You live more by heart feelings than emotion. You make a small fire, but you sit very close to the warm heart feelings.

ELEVEN

WE TALK ABOUT FOUR PARTS OF SELF—BODY, HEART, MIND, AND SPIRIT.

WE TALK ABOUT FOUR PARTS OF GROWING THINGS— ROOT, STALK, FLOWER, AND SEED.

WE TALK ABOUT FOUR DIRECTIONS—WEST, NORTH, EAST, AND SOUTH.

WE TALK ABOUT FOUR MYSTICAL PIERCINGS NECESSARY TO ATTAIN.

But the four parts of the plant are really all one whole thing. The roots below the soil are still part of the stalk and seed, and cannot be separated from the rest of the plant.

Our manifest, body life is likened to the roots dug deep. I have said that there are four directions that relate to parts of our whole self. But I also say that there is really only one direction. It is the one in which you are facing.

When I finished accepting the first Fire Teaching, I was left wondering where the smoke went after it disappeared. It dissipated into the whole. I wondered where mind went upon our dying. It seemed that the smoke passed through the dome of the heavens. It seemed to go beyond mortal perception, except that the aroma of the smoke lingered on the faint and shifting breezes.

It seemed to me then that there is a definite here (below) and a definite there (above). It became clear to me that the dome of the heavens is *the perception of limitation to mortal mind.* Beyond the dome lies the spirit realm. To transcend the dome is to enter the spirit realm.

At the end of the second Fire Teaching, I saw that in our dying, awareness opens and we travel beyond the dome of mortal limitation. We might then weigh ourselves, and the purity of our hearts, against the wholeness of the Spirit in all things—Holy Spirit.

When we die we go beyond the dome, beyond the veil. This is what we strive for in Vision Quest. There seemed to me to be a duality, of manifest and unmanifest being. I wondered about the duality of being even after I began to take journeys. Perhaps even more then. In my teens I had a visionary seeing that one day I would stand beside a light-house at an ocean, and understand this concept. Since I did not live near any oceans, I let it go. This waiting for years, even for decades, for visions to unfold teaches us patience. We must deal with today, not worry over tomorrow. We still plan, or even hope, but not so that we are not in the here and now.

One day, many years after this vision, a woman I had met sent me a picture postcard from where she lived in Florida. It was of a light-house, with the ocean beyond. She wrote that she somehow knew this would be significant to me, so she had sent it along with an invitation to come visit.

When I arrived, I stood on the sandy beach and stared at the light-house and the ocean beyond. I saw the watery distant horizon fade where it met the skies, blending with a perfect balance. Marking the mid-point was the light-house. I was filled with awe at the realization. My friend looked on kindly as tears rolled down my face. I realized that the waters and air are the same substance reflected two ways. Water evaporates from the oceans, forms clouds, falls as rain, and then rises again in vapors.

But it was not the rain-cycle that amazed me. I realized that the wholeness and one-ness represented by the oceans is the same as the vaporous harmony of the spirit realm. One is perceived from the manifest, the other from the ethereal. The light-house beacon is the golden-yellow Light of the center of being, the perception that divides the two realms of harmony and awareness.

The full impact of this realization struck me at once. And so I wept at the simplicity and beauty of the understanding—body and spirit separated only by a perception. The dome of the heavens, limit of mortal awareness, only a perception.

It was a life revelation to me, and I thought of the Christian phrase:

As it is in heaven, so it is on earth.
As it is above, so it is below.

Body, heart, mind, and spirit—all four in harmony and balance, separated only by a perception.

West, north, east, and south—points on the horizon, indicated by the way the sun moves and shines in our lives.

Dream, body, mind, and spirit—indicated by the way the Light moves and shines in our lives.

The only direction is the one in which we are facing. If we are facing body life only, that is the reality we perceive. If we are facing dream, that is the reality of the moment through visions. The other directions and parts of self are always there. We are just looking the other way.

In the body realm, we see and understand only the physical and mental, except for the subtle proddings of our own spirit, perhaps moments of *déjà vu.*

Déjà vu is a moment where your own spirit, existing on its own level all the time, fills your manifest self. To our free spirit-self, our whole body life is like a dream that it once had. When a mystic touches pure spiritual self, he recalls the body life. Thus, he not only sees into the future, he might actually remember the future.

Déjà vu, a moment of feeling as though we had done this before. We almost know what will happen next, and think it must be something wondrous coming. It hardly ever is. It is the intrusion of our very own spirit-self into body life, trying to get us to notice its presence. Our spirit knows what will happen next, most often just mundane events. It is not usually trying to warn us about anything. It is just trying to get us to notice its very existence, and perhaps make us more spiritually aware.

When a person comes into harmony, they need not always have seeings. They can sometimes just make statements with absolute certainty. They just know things because they are in touch with pure Spirit. They can sometimes just know things because they touch pure Spirit while in body.

The direction in which we face is the reality in which we live. To be a mystic is one reality. It is to look at, and from, a particular direction. If we train ourselves to see only logical things and leave no room in our life for mystical things, they can occur right before us but the brain seeks a logical explanation. We could see someone appearing right before us, but since it does not accord with our idea of reality, we dismiss it. We even say to ourselves, "Did that man just appear? No! Couldn't have. I must not have seen him approaching. Yeah, that's it. I just didn't see him coming."

Then, our personal idea of reality restored, we feel safe and secure once more to carry on our lives. If the brain did not leap to a sensible conclusion it would have to admit that our personal idea of reality is just our *idea* of reality. The brain does not like to face such things. Some people pass out at ceremony because they cannot deal with things appearing from nowhere, and the change of consciousness involved.

If you face the direction of ceremonial consciousness, and are priestly in attitude, you are removed from others not on that level. Some people could not deal with being around Grandpa Fools Crow much. I know that I was severely strained at first until I found a consciousness that we were both comfortable with. I had to learn greater periods of silence, until I could just sit with him for hours on end without mental activity, but while maintaining full awareness. Grandpa never taught me this. It just became clear that this was needed, so I strove for it.

It was an education to see all the behavioral traits he had acquired through a lifetime of learning. He always ate quietly. He never talked or chatted. It was almost ritualistic when he ate a meal. He was a silent eater. I saw that while he ate, he kept centered. Most people change perceptions when they eat. He did not. So, I tried it. One starts to eat slower, enjoys the meal more thoroughly, and needs less food for the same nourishment. The value of the food seems to sink right through you. Inner strength is gained through this. No, Grandpa never taught me any lessons. We just hung together. Despite over sixty years difference in our ages, he was one of the closest friends I have had. Fools Crow adopted me in the Lakota way as a grandson, but was a friend more than anything else. It was very educational just to see him at his work.

When certain people came around, Grandpa's stare became piercing—like tiny pieces of coal that could burn right into your soul. He was always centered, but sometimes his intensity was fascinating to see.

If you stay centered like this, you can traverse any spoke of the wheel. You can switch consciousness and go from ceremonial attitude deep into warrior heart. All of these things revolve and swirl around the center. In body life, we live amidst that swirling motion and seek the calm center. From this center, we can emerge in any direction. This is why I say there is only the direction that we are facing. The others are still there, but separated by perception. This also explains being in two realms at once. And being in two places at once. The free-flying spirit is already existing. It intrudes into your night-dreams at times, hinting at what reality might bring as you learn and grow. This is how moonlight reflects sunlight. You dream that you are flying, and in the sunlight you might actually enact what these symbols represent. The things that you do in dream are symbolic of what you might do while awake. We just do not understand the symbols. In body states, we can become aware of the spiritual self. At first we might put body awareness into peaceful rest. We think that consciousness has left the body and traveled somewhere. Eventually, we will find that we are merely switching off body awareness, and getting it out of the way so that we can become aware of the already existing spiritual self.

We find this out because the body can carry on talking and walking around.

It is a shock to the mortal mind, or brain, to learn this. Body consciousness is not all we have. Mortal awareness is not all there is.

While traveling around, if we have reached a higher level of awareness, we can even generate another body in another place and time. Because body life is but a dream it once had, the spirit can choose to have that dream wherever or whenever it finds itself. This is not something I ever sought. I have never sought any one use of the power. I have only sought to grow more Light. To impose our craving and ego-desires on the spiritual perceptions is wrong. This would be to cut, shape, or change the Stones, to desecrate them. It is to change the natural thing to what our human brain thinks things should be like. Whatever happens will be the best that should happen. If I personally never use power again, so be it. Living centered is to generate Light, to be whole and complete. Powers are a side issue.

To leave the body and travel around as a free spirit is to change consciousness levels. It is to change fundamental perceptions. We begin by changing mood, and feelings. Thus, our imagination helps us. We recall how it felt to sit in the old power man's ceremony, or how we felt on Vision Quest. We recall how it felt when the eagles talked to us, or when the mountain lion sat beside us on a cold and lonely night-fast. We recall how it felt to experience a great sign, or when we saw a wonder of the natural world. We know what it feels like to stand in the pines on a crisp, snowy day.

Not hallucinations, not made-up imaginings. This is the creative power that for lack of a better word we call imagination. Creative power is something that we each have. In the manifest realm, we act out spiritual abilities. Instead of learning to talk over distance (telepathy), society has the telephone. We make objects from other materials, and even make new materials. In the realm of spiritual awareness, we also use creative powers. Flying as a sphere of pure Light, we can even generate another solid body—not a mere apparition. We can even create objects, and they stay manifest.

Arriving at this state is sometimes spoken of as having crossed the river to the other side of life. Having done these things, having taken journeys, arriving at the center, we begin to live in both realms. From this mid-point (center) of the two parts of a whole self, we use powers and generate Light.

When Jesus transfigured into pure White Light, He changed consciousness in one swoop while staying in the manifest. Rather than to be aware of two separate realms, He encompassed total awareness while in body. This is the Trans-figuration. Despite the number of mystical events I have seen or been a part of, this remains a deeply mysterious and wonderful thing to me.

All these things may come with expanded awareness, speeded consciousness, and centering. And it is all done straight, with no drugs or hallucinogens.

No matter how far consciousness has expanded, or on which level of self we feel the wholeness and completeness, we are still generating Light. Whether we search the entire cosmos for the mystical rising sun of spiritual illumination, or step outside of our tipi and look up at the sun, we are in Light.

Participating with nature, being in touch with the Spirit in all things, makes us whole. All the levels we reach are already there, existing. We separate ourselves from them by this dome of the heavens, this barrier to perception. We reinforce this barrier by living wrongly. Wholeness and completeness are there all the time.

When we listen to sad music, think of lost loves, we separate ourselves from the feeling of wholeness. Instead, we feel lack. We feel lack because our loved one is not there to help us feel more complete through the Light we generate together. But in Spirit, our loved one is the Light and completeness itself. We separate ourselves from it. How much more sad will we be when the natural world is no longer there to heal our wounds with its wholeness and completeness? Where will human beings turn then? When we feel lost and alone, does the natural world not restore and re-create us?

When I was arriving at setting aside the ego-domination of body self, I was reluctant to surrender to spiritual guidance. I thought that somehow, I would be lost to myself forever. In the end, it was a simple matter of saying yes to Spirit. It is to yield to something higher.

But, as I said, the music that we listen to, the mood that we create within ourselves, acts either to open us up to growth or to close us off from growth. An elder from northern Ontario once explained this to me. I never learned his name. I was traveling to a Native friendship center to visit a friend. This elder saw me approaching. He had been conducting a ceremony there. In the Indian way, he told me, "Change dreams before coming in here."

I asked him how I could possibly do that.

"Start in your feelings . . .

When I entered the center, he was just leaving and greeted me warmly and nodded as we passed. He simply said to me, "Good."

As simple as that. Yet it is a basic tenet of spiritual growth. Begin with your feelings.

Begin with your feelings about yourself. Many people tend to concentrate on the negatives and feel bad about themselves.

Some people think: "I am not good at fixing cars, I can't cook, I have no education, and maybe I am not all that good looking." All this negativity breeds resentments and separates us further from Spirit and Light.

The same person could probably also say, "I can never get lost in the woods, I can hunt and trap, I am honest and live by heart."

If you live by heart, who cares if you can fix cars? Everyone has strengths and weaknesses. Whether we are a contented and strong person depends upon the point we view from. This is the direction where we are standing, viewing. It is perspective, perception. To change our point of view we change our feelings about ourselves, our relation to other people, and our relation to the world. We recall the strong point, not the weak one.

I have been refused service in stores because my braids offended the non-natives. Redneck ranchers have interrupted meals in diners with rude comments about my wife, and by asking me to do a little rain dance for them.

Whether I am content, or sad, depends upon my feelings, and the mood that I create.

I do not have "reservation status." I am not enrolled anywhere. This bothered me for years. It was a dream that I dared not voice aloud. Eventually I learned to let it go. I was waiting for a bus in Rapid City, South Dakota, when an older Lakota came up to me. I had been thinking about all this.

"Nephew! Why are you sad?" (Traditional people sometimes use a family term to indicate brotherhood or compassion.)

"Uncle, I am sad because I do not seem to belong anywhere at all."

"What are you in your heart? Are you Lakota?"

"I am a real Lakota."

"Nephew! Don't worry about a piece of paper saying how Indian you are! We wipe our bum with paper, it is white man's stuff! Paper isn't Indian. Heart is."

A friend of mine in Ontario also has no status. He told me what an elder said to him.

"If we treat you as one of the people and accept you, never mind that you cannot prove blood degree. We know who you are."

I helped someone Vision Quest who had the same problem. So I asked, "Have the Spirits ever asked you for your blood degree before talking to you, or does the Creator ask for your tribal number before giving you a vision?"

It is a point of view, a mood, a feeling.

Likewise, we choose sadness or joy in our lives.

This is part of our creating ability. We can create moods, change feelings, generate Light. Likewise, we choose whether or not we will live with spiritual powers. When we make a decision though we debate and ponder, it always comes out the same. The answer is always yes. We say yes to truth, to Light, to harmony. Here, ego is dealt with.

The ego is partly responsible for helping us to maintain individual being by giving identity and character in the manifest realm. When the ego is too dominant, we grow too dominating and further separate ourselves from Spirit.

The more isolation we feel, the more our inclination towards abuse, or sin against nature and Spirit. The more one lets ego rule the self, the easier the inclination to overemphasize self-importance at other people's cost. This gives rise to lying, stealing, rape, murder, greed, envy, and all the so-called sins. These are manifestations of our separateness from the spiritual whole.

When you live in harmony, you do not seek gain at other people's cost. It is a spiritual consciousness. Goodness is to live within the flowing patterns of the whole, and to be a full part of the Spirit in all things. If attacked, you still defend yourself. If confronted by evil, you still deal with it. You do not seek to do evil, yourself.

243

Living in goodness, you can be holy and still defend yourself. Turning the other cheek only goes so far. There are conditions that demand a further response. Even Jesus caused the fig tree to wither instantly. He did this in the physical. He did not turn the other cheek when He made His belt into a whip and drove the money changers out of the temple. To know when to turn the other cheek is what we must learn. We can only react from the level we inhabit.

Through understanding parts of the whole, and how they interrelate, we understand more of completeness and wholeness. We can also just feel, or sense, the wholeness. When we enter the mystical center of the golden Light, we realize the absolute one-ness of all things on all levels. From this grand understanding, we begin to understand the symbolic values of the parts that make up this vast whole. Though many things are manifested in different forms, through the center we are all connected.

From body realms alone, without spiritual perception, it seems that all things are separate objects. From the pure spiritual awareness of the ethereal void, we know all things are one. The center of these two realms lets us perceive all things as one and whole, yet also maintain enough separateness to be recognized apart from each other.

The center lies between formless ethereal void, and separate solid manifestation. Thus we can perceive ourselves as separate from the rest of creation, and yet all as one. The reason we have a body life at all is to learn and grow aware. In the pure formlessness of void, there is no focused awareness and we cannot separate ourselves from the rest of Creation. This is what we learn in body life.

The Fire Teachings embody this truth. The heat of the Fire and intensity of the flames concentrate and focus awareness. But, we do this in harmony if we wish to grow in spiritual awareness and Light.

As human beings we can become aware of these things. Some of us are called to journey to void and the mystical center. Others are called to live the Fire Teachings and express truth in their daily lives. They are spared the intense pains of ultimate lonely solitude.

Through all the hardships and struggles that we each face in our unique and individual seeking, the same truths are found at each level: centering, wholeness, generating Light. We say:

Make every step a prayer, make every breath a prayer.

Your heart will sing in joy as the fading sun sets for the last time upon your life as a mortal being.

It will have been worthwhile, after all.

TWELVE

THERE HAS ALWAYS BEEN A PLACE IN NATIVE RELIGION FOR THOSE LIKE JESUS.

According to Genesis, God said, "Let there be Light." Then He separated the waters below from the waters above. Later on He created the sun, moon, and stars to light the day and night.

According to the Bible, we are created in God's image. The highest thing, nearest to God, is the Light. First there was only the Creator, and then the Light. In desiring to create, awareness itself was born. The desire to generate Light is the desire to create focused awareness in the formless void. The waters above and the waters below are the ocean and sky symbols. These are the manifest harmony of one-ness which is the Spirit in all things (waters below and oceans) and the ethereal harmony of spiritual awareness (waters above and sky). First was the dome of the heavens separating the spiritual awareness in manifestation from spiritual awareness in the ethereal into two seemingly separate perceptions. Later on, physical rivers and oceans were created.

The waters above and waters below are really one thing, a wholeness and one-ness of spiritual realization. Their dividing line is the barrier to mortal perception.

This is the dome of the heavens we represent by the sweatlodge.

Below all this, later on in creation, came the physical creation of the sun and stars, rivers and oceans. The Light that was created is awareness itself—focus in the timeless and formless void.

In Genesis 1:28, God told human beings to be fruitful and multiply. So, sex was alright and has nothing to do with sin. Sex starts to have to do with sin when craving creates imbalance in us.

After humankind ate the fruit of the tree of knowledge, God said (Genesis 3:22) that now that humans could distinguish good from bad, we should be forbidden the tree of eternal life.

This means that we are not to reach eternal awareness if we can even distinguish good from bad. We must return to living in the harmony of Spirit, perceiving only the good and wholeness in Light. If you are in this Garden-of-Eden consciousness, then all your acts are within the flowing motions of the whole, in touch with the Holy Spirit in all things. This is the Grace of God. According to the Bible, we must return to the innocent wonder of childhood with pure hearts.

After humankind grew wicked and God sent the flood, Noah became a farmer (Genesis 9:20-21). Noah made wine and sat naked in his tent. When he came back to his senses, he cursed the son who was ashamed of his nakedness.

Wine is the ability to go beyond normal body limits and sensations. Clothing is

250

the custom and tradition of our society. If you understand symbols and meanings, you can tell something about a culture from the traditional clothing. Native people in tanned skins represent a different culture with different traditions from Orientals in silks. Noah removed the clothing of custom and tradition and sat naked. He went beyond ordinary awareness. He transcended the dome. Because his son was ashamed and did not understand the significance, and the son was still clinging to old ways, Noah cursed him.

In Genesis 28:10-12, Jacob was traveling and at night lay his head upon a Stone. He dreamed of angels going up and down a ladder or stairway to heaven, and doing the will of the Creator I have always been impressed that he lay his head on a Stone. He rested in a certain perception and consciousness.

In Genesis 37:3, Jacob loved his young son Joseph and gave him a coat (cloak) of many colors. Joseph began to have dreams, and to be able to interpret dreams. He understood the symbolic meanings. The coat, cloak, and robe have the same meaning. In the Native way, it has traditionally been the robe made of an animal's hide. This has been replaced in modern times by the blanket.

These all signify an encapsulating consciousness that we wrap ourselves in. It is a secure perception to protect us and give us heart-warming security. The robe or coat is a dream, a reality, a hue of consciousness from which we use spiritual ability. Joseph's cloak was of many colors, meaning knowledge of many things.

In Exodus 3:2, Moses encountered the burning bush that was not consumed.

He was told that he was on hallowed ground. The bushes and trees are the Standing People. The fact that the bush burned without being consumed symbolizes that Moses would use the great powers without risk of being consumed or tempted by them. He would be a still and calm center though he was afire with power. He would not be consumed by the intensity and great passion needed to use great powers.

Ceremonies existed in the time of the Old Testament. In Exodus 29:1, Jehovah tells how to conduct ceremony to make Aaron and his sons into a priestly line.

In Exodus 20:24-25, Jehovah tells Moses to make only simple altars of softened soil, mellow earth. If one worships through Stone, we are told not to cut, shape, or change the stone in any way. This desecrates it.

We should use the mellow earth teaching of living in harmony. From this consciousness of balance we are worshipping the Creator. If Stone is used, we are not to impose man's ideas upon the fundamental perceptions. Do not change consciousness with the intent of making one particular thing happen to suit your ego. Discover what awaits you. Commune with the one-ness of creation, and you are giving worship to the Creator

When the great mystical prophet Elijah was about to be taken up into heaven, his student Elisha was there. Elijah asked what last favor the student would like granted. Elisha asked for twice the prophet's power Elijah had. Elijah said that if Elisha could actually see the master being taken up to heaven, his wish would be granted. When Elisha saw it, he immediately tore up his own robe and took Elijah's robe for himself. This particular robe signified the spiritual ability Elijah had. This is similar to Joseph's cloak signifying his ability to dream and interpret dreams.

In Genesis 7:17, it rained for forty days and nights, causing the great flood. In Exodus 34:28, Moses was atop the mountain of stone for forty days and nights with no food or water. In Matthew 4:1-2, Jesus went into the wilderness for forty days and nights.

At the end of forty days, Jesus was tempted. He was asked to turn the Stones into bread to ease His hunger. This means to seek the abilities of the fundamental perceptions. He replied that man does not live by bread alone, but by every word coming from the mouth of the Creator, to honor the will of the Creator. This means the great powers of a prophet are not the nourishment we should seek. We must live in the right way, pleasing the will of the Creator and fulfilling sacred design. Stone can nourish us in its way. We learn about Light and Spirit through the different perceptions. To seek just one part of the whole, and isolate it, would be to cut ourselves off from wholeness.

Jesus was transported atop the temple in Jerusalem. He was asked to jump off so the angels could save Him. He replied that we are not to tempt the Creator. He was put atop the religious center, the highest level in the religion. He was asked to jump back down to the level unaware men live at, to see if the angels would rescue and elevate Him again. He replied that we are not to test the Creator by purposely losing ourselves to see if He will find us and save us.

Jesus was transported atop the highest mountain. It represents the highest consciousness that we can reach and still maintain body; it's as high as we can ever climb in the physical. Jesus was told that everything below Him, all the kingdoms and levels below Him, would be His if He would serve evil. Jesus replied that scripture says we must serve the Creator alone, and do His will.

We say nowadays, absolute power can corrupt absolutely. If your heart is pure, corruption cannot get in. Jesus demonstrated that ego-desires had no pull on Him.

In Matthew 5:8, Jesus says, "Blessed are those whose hearts are pure, for they shall see God."

It is difficult in a commercial and capitalistic world to keep your heart pure. There are so many hard-hearted people whose greed destroys the earth, other people's lives, other people's souls. If you have a pure heart, you might seem naïve to hardhearted people. They may try to take advantage of you.

In Matthew 5:13, Jesus tells His disciples they are the world's seasoning, the salt of the earth. Jesus asks them, If you lose your flavor, what will happen in the world?

He says the disciples are the world's light, and the hue of consciousness giving flavor to changing consciousness. They embody the mood and feeling we should acquire in ourselves.

Jesus further tells them they are the world's Light and not to hide their Light under a basket. Let it shine. If the rest of the world has gone wrong, how should they get well again and be whole and complete if there is no one of Light among them? If there is no pure heart among the sinners, how should they change?

Living with a pure heart is difficult in all ages. With the earth so populated it seems more difficult nowadays.

In Matthew 5:23-24, Jesus says that if we are about to worship, and we recall a grudge against someone, go and set it right before worshipping. You cannot worship and be in harmony if your heart or mind are bad against someone. The grace of God is also a pure heart. We are to come before the Creator with a pure heart. If our prayers are to be heard, we must live right.

In Matthew 5:43, Jesus tells us to love our enemies and not hate them. If we are consumed by hate, we further remove ourselves from the Great Spirit. Jesus says that we are to be perfect even as God, our Father, is perfect.

This is exactly where Jesus advises us to dare to aspire to be perfect like Him, perfect like God.

In Luke 11:34, Jesus tells us that our eyes light up our inner being. A pure eye lets in sunshine (the Light), while a lustful eye shuts out Light and plunges us into darkness. If we live right, even our faces will be radiant, as though bathed in Light. This is a degree of the Transfiguration and generating Light from the manifest realm. Old-time Native people also had this. If you look at the earliest pictures of Native people, many seem to shine from within. They lived in harmony and Light.

In John 19:23-24, the soldiers crucifying Jesus divided his clothing among them, but threw dice for his robe. They did not want to rip it up to each get a piece, as it was made without a seam.

Since the robe symbolizes a hue of consciousness and spiritual ability, a robe with no seam means that it was a whole thing. It signifies that the way of Jesus is about wholeness. This is partly what generates Light.

Once you understand symbols, having gone to the center and perhaps even beyond, you can begin to see how these things really relate to each other. All of these things about consciousness, perception, pure heart, and generating Light are in the Bible. They are phrases here and there but once you understand mystic symbology it is an opening of understanding in you.

All Native nations have their own creation teachings. Each is based upon some aspect of truth, a lesson about consciousness and Light. The aspect of the whole truth that is centralized becomes the foundation and doctrine of a Way, its cornerstone. This is the beat of the drum to many Native nations. Christianity is concerned with generating Light. From the first utterance of God, "Let there be Light," to the Resurrection, Transfiguration, and teachings of Christ. Most Native ways are concerned with Heart. This is central to living in harmony, which in turn generates Light.

When unattained people try to interpret Stone Dreams, Fire Teachings, and mystic symbols, they can only make a confused jumble of ego-filled illusions. If you are ruled by ego, how can you judge ego-less-ness?

I was raised Catholic Christian. For twenty years I never heard anyone say that the wine represents the ability to transcend mortal limits. If you think about it, you know that alcohol makes you go beyond normal body senses and awareness. Society has turned from ceremonial wine, taken in the hope of glimpsing Spirit, to sensual wine and seeking body pleasures from altered consciousness.

I have never heard of a priest telling how a member of the parish fasted and transcended. I have never heard of a priest transcending, except for a few who were ignored until after they died. On the other hand, I have had to deal with so-called medicine men who do not hesitate to put medicine on a good-looking woman to sleep with her, even if she is married. Then, they throw her away and do not want her anymore. It might be the exception to the rule, but it happens. The ability to misuse power also exists. We call it evil.

That is why I give you a crucial reason not to misuse spiritual powers. When you die, you will have your life and acts weighed against the purity of the whole. The transition from body life to afterlife will be determined here. If you abuse power, you will be paid back in this life or the next.

Better to be a humble person of good heart, than to have all the power in the world. This is what Jesus said: better to lose the whole world, but gain our soul.

Fame, honor, recognition, money, achievement—these are all but fleeting glimpses of ego admiring itself. Ego is a fickle lover, who will one moment tell you how great you are, but in the next prove to be the weakness that causes your suffering and demise.

We have been misled by thinking of Jesus as God-made-man. Jesus is not the Creator any more than we are. He was a fleshly man with a pure consciousness. His devotion to Light and Spirit were perfect. When we think of Jesus as the Creator made man, come to take away our sins, we are mistaken. Jesus taught how we could seek redemption, enter the grace of God, and participate with the Spirit in all things. He taught how we can generate Light and live in the right consciousness. Jesus said that we should pray to *our* Father, not only His Father. Children of the Light, are children of the same Father. It is wrong to think that somehow Jesus did it all for us. We still have to do it.

When Jesus was crucified, the sky darkened, and the sun (the Light) was blotted out. Great thunder and lightning came. The mysterious power filled the people with awe. Everyone trembled in fear. When Jesus died, the curtain that hides the inner sanctum of the temple was ripped apart from top to bottom. Before this, the inner sanctum of the mystic was the sole domain of the priestly line. Only they could go behind the veil in the temple. Now all the people could see into the mysterious secrets of the temple for the first time. The whole world could look in and see beyond the veil that separates the realms.

Jesus caused the hidden truths to be revealed to the world. We still have to look, to learn, and to live these truths. This is one of the most important things in the Bible, and most churches fail to teach it.

To demonstrate that even those living in darkness, spiritually dead, could be raised up to life and Light, Jesus enacted this truth through giving Himself to death. He rose from the physically dead so we could know anything is possible. It is easier to rise from the spiritually dead.

The Native world has much in common with Old Testament times. There are ceremonies, voices in thunderclouds, water from Stone. People fast, seek visions. There has always been a place in Native religion for those more like Jesus, seeking to live in Light and harmony, beyond the reliance on ritual.

Jesus accepted His role and fulfilled sacred design. In Jesus' time, the Old Testament was just that: old, as in old news. There were others who taught and healed, but the authority of Jesus was unmistakable. People recognized Him.

Today, again, people look at the whole Bible as old news. It is said that many clergy do not even believe that Jesus rose from the dead. In mystical understanding, knowing how we can see into the past and future, and even talk telepathically through time, it is not unthinkable that Jesus could appear again in body. It is not unlikely that it will be in the next fifty years. It could be anytime.

The prophecy is that like lightning flashing in the East and seen at the same time in the West, so will the coming of Jesus be. This means that the second coming will trigger a vast awakening of the population. Lightning is a sudden encompassing burst of Light which startles us into waking up for a moment.

The whole world will suddenly look at its acts—gathering money and fame, ego-cravings, stroking ego—and the whole world could be in dread of judgment. It will be so undeniable that the whole world will know the truth about living in Light, harmony, and heart.

Jesus is also in Native knowledge. At the end of the last century the Ghost Dance movement also concerned itself with Jesus. In the Bible, Jesus is called the Morning Star (Revelation 22:16). The morning star rises before the sun, leading the way. Jesus led the way to Light. The clear Light will come to us from the east, and warm the earth with harmony and contentment.

When Grandpa Fools Crow prayed, he had no objection to including Jesus in the prayers with the Pipe. He also took communion with his wife, Katie.

Churches have concentrated on how to live right in daily life. It's fine as far as it goes. They have not emphasized how we can grow more holy by transcending and generating Light. Many people sense there must be much more than just turning the other cheek, and so they have left organized Christianity behind. It is good that we are told the attributes of holiness, for good works might help us open ourselves to change consciousness. But these single characteristics of holiness must be supplemented by the overall understanding of spiritual development. Churches either do not understand or have chosen to keep this from people.

When I say that Jesus wanted us to be like Him, to be as perfect as the Father in heaven is, I hope you understand this means spiritual development. This is not meant to reduce Jesus in any way. It is meant to elevate us.

We have dug a great pit, and lowered humanity into it. We cannot see beyond that deep, cavernous place of shadows. It is time that we climbed out and looked around at the world of sunlight.

I saw this in my vision as a youth. Between the mountains of stone, and the mountains of snowy pines, was a wide valley floor. It was dry like a desert. From the valley floor, the tops of the mountains seemed like an impossible height. Very few tried to climb the snowy mountains with easy trails. No one tried to scale the sheer stone cliffs of the other mountains. This desert valley held hundreds upon hundreds of thousands of people. They milled forward slowly, indicating the passage of time, the forward progress of humanity. Eventually, the people came to the end of the mountains which bordered the valley. The valley opened out to a plain. Directly ahead of this mass of humanity was a single, low mountain. The sides were steep, but there was a place directly ahead where one could ascend. The great mass of people chose to travel around this mountain. They thought there must be a better place beyond it, hoping for a better way to live. Everything they had known so far was desert.

One small group detached itself from the rest of humanity. They chose to travel alone. Then a few more people left the surging mass of humanity and joined the small group. A few turned back because they feared what may lie beyond the safety of humanity's routines.

The small group climbed slowly up the mountain, not knowing what was up there but trusting the leadership of a very spiritual man. Atop the mountain they found a wide, fertile plain. Thick, lush grasses grew over the wide flat area. The plain seemed to extend forever. It seemed to them as though no other world but this existed. Where the land should have dropped off in cliffs, it extended to distant horizons. There were no cliffs or descents to the valley floor anymore. The place they had left no longer existed for them. They had found a new earth.

This small group of people, retreating to the solitary mountain, discovered the level that humanity was meant to live at.

The main thing that Jesus taught was that we should do the will of the Creator. To discover the will of the Creator, sacred design, we must fast often. Jesus fasted often. He went into natural areas alone to pray.

Whatever the will of the Creator is, is our work on earth. The work that Jesus had was to teach, demonstrate spiritual powers, and to die amidst great and awesome powers.

In the Native way, some are called to be healers, some are prophets. Some live a good, simple, quiet life of generating Light as the Fire Teachings indicate. Whatever we are called to do, we can fulfill the will of the Creator.

Like Jesus, we might know our work from before our birth. We might discover it in early youth, or as a young adult. It might take us forty, even seventy years to find and do our work.

When Uncle Mark told me why he taught me, he said this was part of his vision. He had that vision before I was born. Uncle Mark was also a seer and healer. By doing the work that we are given, we fulfill sacred design. In general, the will of the Creator is that we live in harmony, generate Light, grow whole and complete. To accomplish our work is a great blessing for ourselves, and for humanity.

If we do these things, we are a full part of creation, in the Grace of God, the Great Spirit in all things.

EPILOGUE

The grandeur of life is something that we train ourselves not to perceive when we live removed from the wholeness of the natural world.

When a dark, boiling thundercloud comes sweeping out of the clear western skies, and stops above us, rumbling, we are filled with wonder. When a mighty encompassing voice speaks to us, we are filled with awe. When a blade of soft spring grass brushes against our bare ankle, we may feel the same awe and wonder.

I have told you things from my personal life so that you can know it is really possible. I am a man in a body. This is not a teaching tale from long ago. I am alive today.

We have capabilities that people immersed in technological society do not even imagine. By we, I mean spiritual mystics around the world—and you, too, if you so choose.

There is a great, peaceful feeling at good medicine ceremonies, and when you participate with Spirit. It is a deep knowledge that, somehow:

Everything is alright.

Everything is whole, rounded, and complete.

There might be no food at home, or even no home to go to. There could be no job waiting, but somehow:

Everything is alright, filled and complete.

Everything is in its place. You are in the whole. You touch Spirit and the Grace of God:

Somehow, everything is alright. This is the "sweet medicine."

When you have lost your way, and you feel cold and abandoned in the world, you can climb the mountain and pray. You can be taken back into wholeness and Spirit once more. It is as though your ignoring Spirit for a while was a sin that has been forgiven, and once again:

Everything is alright.

You feel the warmth and fullness of heart, and Light shines within you.

The Spirit never shuts you out. You remove yourself from its touch. The awe and wonder of creation is that if we seek to re-enter the wholeness and light, we may do so. It feels much like having sins forgiven. Jesus also said, "Be whole, and sin no more." Is sin, then, not a result of having separated ourselves from the Holy Spirit in all things, and the whole?

For all the thunderstorms, healings, miracles, and mystic signs, one of the greatest things is that we can re-enter this touching of Holiness of Life, this Great Holy Spirit in all things, including in us.

This is healing. It is the true healing that counts.

To me:

It is the wonder and awe of Life.